GALE GAND'S
Lunch!

GALE GAND'S
Lunch!

Gale Gand

with Christie Matheson

Photographs by Ben Fink

Houghton Mifflin Harcourt
Boston • New York • 2014

For information about permission to reproduce selections
from this book, write to Permissions, Houghton Mifflin
Harcourt Publishing Company, 215 Park Avenue South,
New York, New York 10003.

www.hmhco.com

Library of Congress Cataloging-in-Publication Data

Gand, Gale.
Gale Gand's lunch! / Gale Gand with Christie Matheson ;
photographs by Ben Fink.
     p. cm.
Includes index.
ISBN 978-0-544-22650-0 (cloth); 978-0-544-18650-7 (ebk)
1. Luncheons. 2. Natural foods. I. Matheson, Christie. II. Title.
TX735.G36 2013
641.5'4—dc23
                    2013019526

Interior design by Laura Palese
Printed in China

TOP 10 9 8 7 6 5 4 3 2 1

A12006 363235

This book is dedicated to my sweet and loving husband, Jimmy Seidita, who always seems willing to put up with my crazy busy life, and to my three children, Giorgio Montana Gand Tramonto, Ella Nora Gand Seidita, and Ruby Grace Gand Seidita, who inspire me, give me a reason to cook, and celebrate in the kitchen with me daily. Thanks, you guys, for tasting everything I make. (Well, except for one of you, and you know who you are!)

Contents

Introduction

I've always loved making lunch for my family and my friends. But for a long time, I rarely, if ever, made it for myself—unless I was planning to eat with someone else.

I spend my days and nights feeding others, but it didn't occur to me to take care of myself in the same way. Then one day, when I was up early packing a lunch box for my son before I went to work, I thought about how nice it would be to eat a homey noontime meal. So I assembled one for myself too. That turned out to be a very good idea, because I was heading into a *long* day.

Of course, there are many long workdays in the life of a chef. It's typical for me to start before dawn and work all day preparing bread and pastries, or to spend countless hours on set taping a television show or teaching classes. But for some reason that particular day felt like one of the longest ever. By noon, I was exhausted, even jittery—and very hungry. Contrary to popular belief, chefs don't snack endlessly on the things they make. At least I don't! There's no time for that.

I had an opportunity for a twenty-minute break, and that's when I remembered, joyfully, my homemade lunch. It wasn't elaborate: a portion of three-bean chili (plus a tiny container of grated cheese and a small baggie of homemade croutons for sprinkling on top), a clementine, and a bottle of raspberry kefir. Having that food waiting for me truly made my day. Made. My. Day.

The meal, with its contrasting flavors and textures (warm, hearty soup; cheese that melted as I stirred it in; crunchy croutons; a bright, citrusy clementine; and the creamy yet tangy yogurt drink) was incredibly satisfying. It provided real nourishment, and gave me a proper break. I was *much* more productive after eating, thanks to a simple lunch that had taken me just a few minutes to throw together. I simply pulled out a portion of chili from my freezer, grabbed a handful of croutons I'd made in advance, added the clementine, and tossed in a bottle of kefir. The step that took the longest was grating the cheese. (And of course you can buy that already grated.) The effort was more than worth it.

And now I'm committed to teaching others how wonderful and easy it can be to make lunch. It doesn't have to take much time, and I strongly believe that all of us—kids and adults alike—are significantly more fulfilled by homemade food than meals composed of highly processed, barely perishable, stale vending machine items. I'm not the only one who thinks so.

One of the hottest food topics in the nation right now—from schools to celebrity chefs' kitchens all the way to the White House—is lunch. Food lovers around the country are devoting themselves to the quest to make delicious, nourishing lunches available to everyone. Whether we pack lunch for our kids to take to school or for ourselves to take to work, or make lunch for friends coming over, or prepare some things to put in a basket for a picnic, or simply throw something together to eat at home, we all eat lunch. There's no reason why that meal can't be wonderful, good for you, and varied from day to day.

If you're going to toss together a turkey sandwich, why not make it mouthwatering by adding arugula and mango chutney? Instead of plain old chicken salad, how about chicken salad punctuated by the sweetness of dried cranberries, the crisp, subtle flavor of fennel, and the crunch and nuttiness of toasted almonds? It really doesn't take any longer to prepare. Likewise, recipes such as Pea and Garlic Dip or Roasted Beets and Carrots with Orange couldn't be easier to make— and don't they sound more appealing than the same old cafeteria lunch? If someone invited you to her house for lunch and there was a fragrant bowl of summer tomato soup with basil and Parmesan cream waiting for you alongside a platter of grilled three-cheese sandwiches, you'd be pretty happy, right?

Some of my fondest food memories are of wonderful lunches. One of the most perfect meals I've ever had was a lunch at a friend's house. We ate a Spanish tortilla, which was simply thinly sliced potatoes and onions poached in olive oil then folded into beaten eggs and cooked on the stove in a skillet. We ate it with bacon, bagels, and fruit salad. Nothing fancy, and yet I can't get it out of my head. The experience was the perfect combination of delicious food, a colorful table, sunlight, and wonderful company. There was just enough food, but not too much, and a balance of salty and sweet menu items. It was simple, yet sophisticated in its simplicity—and that only would have been possible at lunchtime, when expectations are relaxed, the time commitment is less, and the pressure that exists with a dinner party is entirely absent. As a guest and as a host you probably have more energy at lunchtime. Because entertaining at lunchtime is so much easier, I think lunch should be the new dinner.

The best parties I've ever hosted have been lunch parties—big outdoor summer lunches, sometimes with the grill on, and once with a mouthwatering assortment of creative sandwiches (or, as I usually call them, sammies): decadent lobster rolls; little rolled sandwiches filled with roasted eggplant spread; and Mexican chicken salad sandwiches with a kick of spice and a dose of creamy avocado. With the sandwiches we also served a zesty chilled gazpacho, mango lemonade (gin optional), and iced tea. And I made devil dogs, a chocolate devil's food cake sandwiched with a cream filling, so even dessert was a type of sandwich. That's not the kind of food you'd expect at a dinner party, but let's be honest: Isn't it the type of food you really love?

My kids certainly love it, and I enjoy sending them to school with wonderful things in their backpacks or trying new lunch foods with them at home. I never have any problem getting them to eat vegetables, fruits, and other healthy foods at lunchtime. Presented simply in sandwiches, soups, or on their own, they are tremendously appealing.

It can be so easy to make amazing lunch food—all you need are good ingredients and some inspired ideas. That's why I'm sharing more than 150 lunch-perfect recipes in *Gale Gand's Lunch!*

I've long been a proponent of making healthy, interesting lunches, and I've been preparing lunch for my children to take to school every day for years. These days I also love making lunch for myself, whether I'm eating at home or packing it to go.

When I'm in the middle of a long workday, or if I'm traveling, having a homemade lunch to look forward to is such a treat. I adore entertaining at lunchtime too. And sometimes my husband, Jimmy, and I go on "mystery dates" to the park or the beach. He's in charge of planning the destination and our itinerary and I pack the picnic lunch. Those have been some of our best dates ever!

In *Gale Gand's Lunch!* you'll find plenty of fun and creative ideas for lunch, including simple recipes for lunchtime snacks, pastas, salads, sammies, soups, drinks, condiments, and more—and lots of ideas for mixing and matching them, whether you're taking them to go, eating at home, or throwing a lunchtime party.

Breakfast may have the reputation of being the most important meal of the day, but I believe lunch is the meal most of us actually do eat every day, whether we're kids eating in the school cafeteria, grown-ups grabbing a bite at our desks, or friends having lunch together. Let's make lunch healthier, more meaningful, and more delicious. It's easy!

Lunch is also a great time to entertain simply. It's a quicker meal that generally features less expensive ingredients than those used for a dinner. It can be completely flexible and family friendly, and it doesn't require much work to make an impressive lunch (in part because expectations aren't as high as they are for dinner, and there are fewer "rules" that you need to follow). If you simply have a main course salad at lunch, that's fine! Making lunch well is all about using great ingredients, rather than involved techniques. As I entertain at lunchtime more and more often, I find that people seem to respond incredibly well to this kind of food. And I like that it excuses me from having to make complicated things.

And yet so many of us, and so many of our kids, aren't eating lunches made from great ingredients—they're getting preservative-laden, processed, packaged foods that may have been sitting on grocery store shelves for months—or even years. This just isn't a healthy way to eat. And making healthy lunches doesn't have to be much more difficult. I've been a "culinary cop" for ten years, making my way into school lunchrooms to see what parents are packing, and it crushes me to see what most kids are eating for lunch. (I think that if a food grows *on* a plant, you should eat more of it; if it's made *in* a plant, you should eat less of it.) By making lunch out of fresh ingredients, you're teaching kids to have a better relationship with food.

I would hate to think the reason my kids get requests for play dates is because of the lunches I make them when their friends come over, but I'm beginning to wonder. When I walk into one of my kids' classrooms, I'm inundated with requests for play dates, and the request always ends with, ". . . and will you make that grilled

cheese you made last time?" I even get emails from moms asking for the secret to my grilled cheese sandwiches, because their kids are asking them to make it like Ruby and Ella's mom does. So whenever we have kids over for play dates (and since I have twins, we try to do double ones), I'm making my signature grilled cheese (with a combination of cheeses and gently pan-grilled oat bread) for four hungry, happy kids. I serve fresh fruit and veggies on the side, and I always take a picture of the kids at the table and send it to the moms so they can feel connected to where their kids were and what they ate that day.

In June 2010, First Lady Michelle Obama invited me to the White House garden to help kick off her "Chefs Move to Schools" campaign, which is aimed at reducing childhood obesity by bringing healthier food into our schools for our kids' lunches, and making food—real food—more a part of the educational system by bringing it into the classrooms for lessons. I teach cooking and nutrition at schools in the Chicago area, often going into a French class (and using cooking to teach the language) or an outdoor adventure class (part of the physical education curriculum), or into regular classes, just to give kids some hands-on experience with cooking by making something simple, like fresh spring rolls.

Making lunch at home is a great money saver, whether you pack a lunch to take to the office or make it for your kids. It's also a more affordable and flexible—and less formal—way to entertain. And it certainly makes sense as a daily habit for those who work from home or telecommute. Given the state of the economy for the past few years, I am certainly cost-conscious these days, and so are most people I know. We are turning to homemade foods instead of restaurants as a way to ease stress on the wallet. A recent survey found that 35 percent of employees made it a financial goal last year to bring lunch from home instead of buying it—because, as the same survey showed, buying lunch costs an average of almost $2,000 per year. With the recession still looming, people will be making lunch at home even more often in years to come. Now is the perfect time for a book filled with delicious, easy, and creative recipes for lunch!

I've said this before, and I know I'll mention it again: Using fresh, local, seasonal ingredients (and organic, if possible) can make preparing food so much easier. If you use great ingredients, you need to do less to make a meal taste delicious. And buying local reduces the "food miles," or amount of energy needed to get your ingredients to you, which reduces the ultimate cost of the food.

Aside from fresh, local ingredients, I also have a list of staples that I stock in my pantry. I'm a chef, so this is a long list! Here are some items for you to consider, so you can pick and choose what makes sense for you. I always have canned beans, chickpeas, cranberry sauce, clam sauce, cocoa powder, chicken broth, and canned corn. In jars I have peanut butter, Nutella, myriad mustards, artichokes, olives, pickles, jams, marmalades, and tomato sauce. In bottles I have oils (canola, olive, sesame), soy sauce, vinegars (red wine, white wine, apple cider, rice wine, balsamic), ketchup, maple syrup, Tabasco, and Worcestershire sauce. Dry items include a few different types of rice, a dozen types of pasta (but remember, my husband's Italian), dried beans and peas, panko bread crumbs, barley, wheat berries, farro, quinoa, two kinds of couscous, and cornmeal.

In my fridge I have cheeses, including grated Parmesan to add to biscuits, a block of Parmesan for grating over pasta, sliced American and Muenster, a log of goat, fresh mozzarella (usually in the smaller ball sizes, or "bocconcini," for easy snacking), grated cheddar for sprinkling over soups and chili, and cream cheese. There's also yogurt, cottage cheese, and unsalted butter in the fridge, and some butter out at room temperature next to the toaster. I buy low-fat milk for drinking and whole milk for tea.

My spice bin contains half sweeter spices, like cinnamon, ginger, vanilla, and nutmeg, and half savory spices, like paprika, thyme, bay leaves, and cumin. I use a pepper grinder filled with a mix of peppercorns (black, green, pink, and white—which are just black peppercorns without the peel) and sometimes juniper berries in the mix, and I keep it on the stove next to my salt shaker, which is filled with kosher salt. I don't keep kosher, even though I'm Jewish, but I do like how the snowy flakes of salt sprinkle compared to iodized table salt.

I recommend having a small serrated knife for cutting sammies and a small offset spatula for spreading fillings. You'll also need basic measuring cups and spoons and a few good pots and pans (I like to have 2-quart, 3-quart, and 4-quart pans with lids, a 6-quart pot for making soup, and sauté pans in two different sizes, like 8-inch and 10- or 12-inch). Always useful are scissors, a nonabsorbent cutting board, decent knives, tongs, an egg slicer, slotted spoons, wooden spoons, and a lemon juicer (the kind that looks like a giant garlic press). Bigger equipment that I use often includes small roasting pans, baking sheets, food processor, stand mixer, blender, colander, and my trusty panini press (I really think everyone should have one of those!).

For packed lunches and picnics, I have heavy (reusable!) plastic forks and spoons, lightweight reusable containers with lids (some with multiple compartments), resealable bags, bento boxes, a picnic basket, thermoses, lightweight, unbreakable plates and cups, cloth lunch boxes or reusable lunch bags, and washable napkins.

One of my favorite ways to keep lunches cold is to keep juice boxes frozen and use them in place of ice packs. The juice box should thaw by lunchtime, and it keeps things cool until then. When you're sending reusable containers to school with your kids, it's a good idea to put their name on the bottom and the top of the containers so everything makes it back home. (I like to put a note in there too, or a joke, to connect with my kids when I'm not with them all day.)

If I'm at home around midday, I love creating an impromptu lunch. Even if you think there's nothing in the fridge or pantry to make for lunch, your inner chef can come out and save the day. Look for one ingredient you can build a dish around, like precooked chicken or pork, and then go from there. I sometimes ask myself what needs to be used up, for inspiration. I'll see two or three things that really need to be eaten, maybe in such small amounts that alone they aren't anything much. But together they might be something. Suddenly I've got a combination that makes sense, and I'm on the culinary road to a fabulous lunch dish. Don't be afraid to get creative at lunchtime.

No matter what you make or where you eat it, I hope you enjoy your lunch!

Acknowledgments

For all the help, support, and kitchen assistance, thanks to: Christie Matheson; Justin Schwartz; Ben Fink; Tom Hamilton; Jane Dystel; my father, Bob Gand; my Aunt Greta and Uncle Robert; my brother, Gary, and his wife, Joan; Joan's mother, Harriet Burnstein; my mother-in-law, Vita Seidita; my sister-in-law, Fran Seidita; our family friend Lana Rae Goldberg; my high school intern, Jess Dawson; the Hearty Boys (Dan Smith and Steve McDonagh); Kathy Skutecki; Elizabeth Brown; Ina Pinkney; Michelle Doll; Sofia Graham; my girlfriends Karen Katz, Janine Gray, Judy Anderson, Marthe Hess Young, Kathy Merritt, Maggie Logan, Franzie Weyer, and my French *amie* Muriel Hamon-Montias; my ex-husbands, Rick Tramonto and Brian Bram; Rich Melman and Lettuce Entertain You Ent.; and the Food Network.

Snacks

Baked Kale Chips

Parmesan–Black Pepper Popcorn

Crispy Roasted Chickpeas

Roasted Rosemary Cashews

Cinnamon Pecans

Gale's Trail Mix

Chive Crackers

Cumin-Spiced Pita Chips

Simple Pickles

Tomato, Cucumber, & Mozzarella Skewers

Dates with Goat Cheese

Homemade Banana Chips

Cheesy Focaccia Sticks

Baked Kale Chips

SERVES 4

These are delicious and crunchy, like very thin potato chips, but much better for you. They're a fantastic snack any time, a fun nosh with a drink, and a great garnish for soups and salads because they add textural variety and some extra nutrition. I came up with this as a result of my overly ambitious garden—I always seem to plant too much kale. Luckily it's pretty in flower arrangements too!

10 curly kale leaves

¼ cup extra-virgin olive oil

¼ teaspoon salt

3 grinds black pepper

PACK IT TO GO WITH:
Cheese cubes and yellow cherry tomatoes

EAT IT AT HOME WITH:
Tomato basil soup, using the kale chips as a crunchy garnish

MAKE IT A PARTY WITH:
Tomato, Cucumber, & Mozzarella Skewers (page 37), Crispy Roasted Chickpeas (page 23), and Chianti Spritzers (page 241)

Heat the oven to 400 degrees.

Remove the stems from the kale leaves with scissors. Cut the trimmed leaves in half crosswise. Set the top halves aside. The spines of the bottom halves are a bit too thick for chips, so remove them by folding the leaves in half lengthwise and cutting the spine out, leaving the leafy part.

Place the kale leaves in a large bowl and toss them with the olive oil, rubbing the oil into the front and back of the leaves and coating them well. There shouldn't be any dry-looking spots. Sprinkle the leaves lightly with the salt and pepper. Arrange the leaves in a single layer on a baking sheet and bake them for about 5 minutes to dry them out. The leaves should feel crisp at the end of the baking time; if they don't, return them to the oven for 1 to 2 minutes more, keeping a close eye on them to make sure they don't burn. Let the chips cool completely on the baking sheet before serving. Store the kale chips in an airtight container or resealable bag at room temperature for up to 1 week.

Parmesan–Black Pepper Popcorn

MAKES ABOUT 6 CUPS

When I was in college at the Cleveland Institute of Art, I was a pretty typical starving art student. I was forced to be extremely economical in my food choices—and I even found a job waiting tables at a restaurant so I could get the free staff meal. This is one of the snacks I started making during that time, and I still make it today!

¼ cup popcorn kernels (about 6 heaping cups popped)

1½ tablespoons unsalted butter, melted

3 tablespoons freshly grated Parmesan cheese

½ teaspoon freshly ground black pepper

¼ teaspoon salt

PACK IT TO GO WITH:
Gale's Gazpacho (page 97)

EAT IT AT HOME WITH:
Roasted Vegetable Salad (page 194)

MAKE IT A PARTY WITH:
Bell Pepper and Blistered Corn Salsa (page 46), corn chips, and Mango Lemonade (page 238)

Place the popcorn kernels in a hot-air popcorn popper and pop into a large bowl.

Toss the hot popcorn with the melted butter. Sprinkle the Parmesan, pepper, and salt over the buttered popcorn and toss to coat well, making sure the cheese doesn't settle in the bottom of the bowl. Let cool, then serve immediately or store in a resealable bag at room temperature for up to 3 days (the popcorn starts to get a little soggy on day 3).

Crispy Roasted Chickpeas

SERVES 4

My husband is crazy about chickpeas. Every time he eats a salad that doesn't have chickpeas in it, he says, "You know, it'd be even better with chickpeas." So we are never without them in our pantry, and sometimes I stockpile so many cans that our shelves get overrun. That's when I make this healthy snack. This mix of spices is delicious, and you can play around with other combinations too! Try curry with a touch of cayenne, or dried oregano and garlic powder.

One 15-ounce can chickpeas

1 tablespoon plus 2 teaspoons extra-virgin olive oil

¼ teaspoon salt

¼ teaspoon ground cumin

¼ teaspoon smoked paprika

¼ teaspoon freshly ground black pepper

Heat the oven to 400 degrees. Line a rimmed baking sheet with paper towels.

In a colander, drain and rinse the chickpeas. Remove as much water as you can, then pour the chickpeas onto the lined baking sheet and place another paper towel on top of them. Roll the chickpeas around between the towels to dry the chickpeas and remove some of their loose, thin skins. Remove the paper towels (from the top and bottom) and add the olive oil, tossing to coat well. Roast the chickpeas for 30 to 40 minutes, until they are golden brown and crispy.

Meanwhile, combine the salt, cumin, paprika, and pepper in a small bowl. Remove the chickpeas from the oven and immediately sprinkle them with the spice mixture, tossing to distribute the mixture and evenly coat the chickpeas. Let cool before serving. The chickpeas will keep in an airtight container at room temperature for up to 2 weeks.

PACK IT TO GO WITH:
Mexican Chicken Salad (page 175)

EAT IT AT HOME WITH:
Turkey with Mango-Tomato Chutney sandwich (page 75)

MAKE IT A PARTY WITH:
Summer Garden Vegetable Soup (page 100) and Simple Green Salad (page 180)

Roasted Rosemary Cashews

MAKES 2 CUPS

These are a little savory, a little sweet, and loaded with energy and flavor. They're great for tiding over guests at the beginning of a lunch party or for packing in lunch boxes. They are so tasty that I definitely advise sharing them with friends, but be sure to reserve some for yourself.

1 tablespoon chopped fresh rosemary

2 teaspoons honey

1 teaspoon salt

⅛ teaspoon cayenne pepper

1 tablespoon unsalted butter, melted

2 cups roasted cashews

PACK IT TO GO WITH:
Copperwell Noodles (page 136)

EAT IT AT HOME WITH:
Dried Fruit Salad (page 202)

MAKE IT A PARTY WITH:
Grilled Orange-Garlic Shrimp Skewers (page 145) and Roasted Vegetable Salad (page 194)

Heat the oven to 350 degrees.

In a medium bowl, mix together the rosemary, honey, salt, and cayenne. Add the butter and toss to combine. Add the cashews and toss well to coat completely. Turn the cashews out onto a baking sheet and bake until the nuts start to brown a little, about 10 minutes. Let them cool completely before serving or storing. The cashews will keep in an airtight container or resealable bag at room temperature for up to 2 weeks or in the freezer for up to 2 months. To defrost, let the cashews thaw in their container at room temperature overnight. Toast them for 10 minutes at 350 degrees if they seem a little soggy.

Cinnamon Pecans

MAKES 2 CUPS

These easy-to-make and slightly addictive pecans are good for snacking, adding to salads, or sprinkling on yogurt or ice cream. They also make a great nibble with cocktails. The combination of orange and cinnamon is my favorite for pecans, but I also like playing around with hints of ginger, clove, or nutmeg to vary the flavor. I encourage you to try different spices too!

³/₄ cup sugar

1 teaspoon grated orange zest

¹/₄ teaspoon ground cinnamon

¹/₄ teaspoon salt

2 cups pecan halves

In a deep saucepan, combine the sugar, orange zest, cinnamon, salt, and ¹/₃ cup water, and bring the water to a boil over medium-high heat. Add the pecans and cook, stirring frequently, until the water has evaporated. The glaze will be shiny and transparent at first, then turn opaque and appear frosted as the water evaporates. When the nuts are completely coated with sugar crystals, quickly spread them out on a baking sheet to cool completely. Store the cooled pecans in an airtight container at room temperature for up to 2 weeks.

PACK IT TO GO WITH:
Butternut Squash and Apple Soup (page 104)

EAT IT AT HOME WITH:
Late Summer Fruit Salad (page 207)

MAKE IT A PARTY WITH:
Mustard-Glazed Pork Tenderloin (page 146), Simple Green Salad (page 180), and Cranberry Almond Coconut Bars (page 213)

Gale's Trail Mix

MAKES 4 CUPS

I like to keep a little of this mix with me (especially on days I know will be long and busy) so I have some quick energy in my pocket when I need it. It's handy when I'm in a meeting, prepping in the kitchen, on a walk with the dog, or out running errands with my kids on the weekends. I like using an assortment of nuts and seeds, in different shapes and colors, such as walnuts, whole cashews, hazelnuts, and sunflower seeds. I try to vary my dried fruit the same way—I've used dried kiwi, dried mango, and dried cranberries.

1 cup granola clusters (such as Trader Joe's)

½ cup whole almonds

½ cup pecans, toasted (see Note)

½ cup roasted salted peanuts

½ cup pepitas (pumpkin seeds)

½ cup dried cherries

½ cup chopped dried apricots

½ cup dried pineapple chunks

½ cup chopped dried apple slices

PACK IT TO GO WITH:
yogurt; stir in the trail mix at lunchtime

EAT IT AT HOME:
sprinkled on oatmeal

MAKE IT A PARTY WITH:
PB&J sandwiches (page 77) made with Apple Butter (page 57) and cut into tea sandwiches, and Chicken and Dumpling Soup (page 110)

Combine the granola, almonds, pecans, peanuts, pepitas, cherries, apricots, pineapple, and apple in a bowl and mix well. The trail mix keeps in an airtight container at room temperature for up to 2 weeks.

Note: To toast nuts, heat the oven to 350 degrees. (Most people toast nuts at a higher temperature, but I find they can easily get away from me and burn, so this temperature is safer.) Place the nuts in a single layer on a baking sheet and toast for about 15 minutes. I check the nuts every 5 minutes and give them a toss so they toast evenly.

Chive Crackers

MAKES ABOUT 2 DOZEN

My friend Paul Kahan, executive chef and partner at Blackbird, avec, and Publican in Chicago, made these crackers for a fund-raiser where we cooked with thirty-eight other chefs. The crackers were so good that I couldn't stop eating them. Paul invited me to visit his kitchen at Publican one day so his pastry chef could teach me how to make them. I've adapted the recipe for home cooks, and though it's not quite the same, it's close—and still delicious. This recipe takes more time than many in this book, but the results are worth it. (And if you want, you can double the recipe.)

1½ teaspoons dry yeast

4 cups all-purpose flour, plus more for your work surface

1 teaspoon sugar

3½ teaspoons salt

1 teaspoon chopped fresh chives

1 teaspoon chopped fresh tarragon

¼ cup extra-virgin olive oil, plus more for the baking sheet and brushing on the dough

1 teaspoon freshly ground black pepper (optional)

Using a wooden spoon and a large bowl or the bowl of a stand mixer fitted with the paddle attachment, mix the yeast, 1½ cups of the flour, and the sugar together with 1¼ cups water to make a sponge (see Note, page 29). Cover the bowl well with plastic wrap and place it in a warm spot in your kitchen (such as above your oven, or turn your oven on low for 10 minutes, then turn it off and use it as a "proof box" for the sponge). Let the sponge sit for about 2 hours, until it triples in bulk.

Add the remaining 2½ cups flour, 1½ teaspoons of the salt, the chives, tarragon, and olive oil directly to the sponge and mix the dough with a wooden spoon (or a stand mixer fitted with the dough hook) to combine well. Cover the dough with plastic wrap again and let it rise for about 1 hour, until doubled in bulk.

PACK IT TO GO WITH:
Roasted Eggplant Spread (page 49)

EAT IT AT HOME WITH:
Pea and Garlic Dip (page 55)

MAKE IT A PARTY WITH:
Greek Potato-Garlic Schmear (page 53), Dilled Green Beans (page 33), and sliced cured sausages

recipe continues

Punch down the dough and wrap the bowl with plastic wrap or a damp tea towel. Chill the dough for about 2 hours to slow down the proofing. This helps develop the flavor, and makes the dough easier to roll out.

Heat the oven to 400 degrees. Brush a baking sheet with olive oil until well coated.

Punch the dough down again and turn it out onto a floured work surface. Using a rolling pin, roll out the dough into very thin, long sheets, like sheets of pasta for lasagna, and place the sheets on the oiled baking sheet. Poke holes all over the sheets of dough with a fork to allow steam to escape during baking. Brush the cracker sheets with more olive oil and sprinkle with the remaining 2 teaspoons salt (and the pepper, if you like). Bake for 20 to 25 minutes, until golden brown. Let the crackers cool on the pan, then break the sheets into 3- to 4-inch shards of cracker. Store the crackers in a resealable bag at room temperature for up to 1 week.

Note: A sponge is a loose, wet mixture, usually made from water, yeast, and flour, used as a starter for a bread or cracker recipe. It's allowed to sit and ferment, which gives extra depth and flavor to the dough. More flour is usually added later to stiffen the dough. Sometimes something like sugar or honey is added to feed the yeast.

Cumin-Spiced Pita Chips

SERVES 6 TO 8

If you're going to make hummus from scratch (see page 51), it's nice to make your own pita chips too. That way you can flavor them with whatever you want: salt and black pepper, paprika and garlic, or cumin, as I do here. I love this version, and I encourage you to try it. Then try coming up with your own personal pita chip flavor.

Four 6- or 7-inch rounds pita bread (with or without pockets)

2 tablespoons extra-virgin olive oil

1 teaspoon salt

2 teaspoons ground cumin

PACK IT TO GO WITH:
Hummus (page 51)

EAT IT AT HOME WITH:
Salsa Verde (page 48)

MAKE IT A PARTY WITH:
Gale's Guacamole (page 50) and Four-Bean Vegetable Chili (page 102)

Heat the oven to 350 degrees.

Cut each pita round into 8 triangles, then if you're using pocket pita bread, open each triangle and break it in half at the fold so you have just one layer of bread instead of two. Place the triangles in a single layer on a large baking sheet and sprinkle them as evenly as possible with about half the oil, then about half the salt, then about half the cumin. Toss the triangles to distribute the spices, spread them back into an even layer, if necessary, then sprinkle them with the remaining oil, salt, and cumin. Bake for 20 minutes, turning the triangles on the sheet and rotating the sheet in the oven halfway through the cooking time to ensure even toasting. Let cool completely on the pan before eating or storing. The pita chips keep in a resealable bag at room temperature for up to 5 days.

Simple Pickles

Pickling can be so easy, and it's a great way to show off your kitchen creativity. It's also an excellent way to preserve many vegetables—not just cucumbers!—when they are at their peak. Here are three basic pickling recipes with different flavor profiles: Asian spiced, dilled, and sweet and sour. They go beautifully with cold meats like salami or pâté and are nice with artisanal cheeses too. Bring them along with your lunch for a crunch fix! All three recipes can be doubled or tripled.

Dilled Green Beans

MAKES ABOUT 5 CUPS

1 pound fresh green beans, ends trimmed

1 cup white wine vinegar

¼ teaspoon crushed dried red pepper

1 tablespoon snipped fresh dill, or
    1 teaspoon dried dill

1 teaspoon salt

1 teaspoon sugar

2 cloves garlic, sliced

Bring a pot of salted water (1 teaspoon salt per 6 cups water) to a boil over high heat. Add the green beans and cook for 4 minutes. Drain the green beans and place them in a heatproof container with a lid, but don't cover them yet.

In a saucepan, combine the vinegar, crushed red pepper, dill, salt, sugar, and garlic with 1 cup water. Bring to a boil over high heat, then reduce the heat to medium and cook for 1 minute. Pour the hot liquid over the green beans and let cool to room temperature, about 1 hour. Cover the container and chill the green beans at least overnight (the longer you leave them, the better the flavor) before serving. The green beans will keep in an airtight container in the refrigerator for up to 4 months.

Asian-Spiced Pickled Carrots

MAKES ABOUT 5 CUPS

1 pound carrots (about 6 medium carrots), peeled

1 tablespoon whole fresh cilantro leaves

One 2-inch piece fresh ginger root, peeled and sliced ⅛ inch thick

3 cloves garlic, peeled and quartered

1 cup rice wine vinegar

3 tablespoons light brown sugar

8 whole black peppercorns

1 teaspoon salt

1 or 2 dried red chiles

Bring a pot of salted water (1 teaspoon salt per 6 cups water) to a boil over high heat. Cut the carrots on the bias to make oval slices about ¼ inch thick. Add the carrots to the boiling water and cook for 4 minutes. Drain the carrots and place them in a heatproof container with a lid, but don't cover them yet. Add the cilantro leaves to the container.

In a saucepan, combine the ginger, garlic, vinegar, sugar, peppercorns, salt, and chiles with 1 cup water. Bring to a boil over high heat, then reduce the heat to medium and cook for 1 minute. Pour the hot liquid over the carrots and let cool to room temperature, about 1 hour. Cover the container and chill the carrots at least overnight (the longer you leave them, the better the flavor) before serving. The pickled carrots will keep in an airtight container in the refrigerator for up to 6 months.

Sweet-and-Sour Pickled Asparagus

MAKES ABOUT 5 CUPS

1 pound asparagus
1 ½ cups cider vinegar
¼ cup sugar
2 shallots, peeled and sliced

1 tablespoon yellow mustard seeds
1 teaspoon whole black peppercorns
1 teaspoon celery seeds
1 teaspoon coriander seeds

Bring a pot of salted water (1 teaspoon salt per 6 cups water) to a boil over high heat. Trim the woody ends off the asparagus, then peel the bottom halves of the stalks with a vegetable peeler. (You may cut the stalks to fit your container if you like.) Add the asparagus to the boiling water and cook for 3 minutes. Drain the asparagus and place the stalks in a heatproof container with a lid, but don't cover them yet.

In a saucepan, combine the vinegar, sugar, shallots, mustard seeds, peppercorns, celery seeds, and coriander seeds with ½ cup water. Bring to a boil over high heat, then reduce the heat to medium and cook for 1 minute, stirring to dissolve the sugar. Pour the hot liquid over the asparagus and let cool to room temperature, about 1 hour. Cover the container and chill the asparagus at least overnight (the longer you leave them, the better the flavor) before serving. The pickled asparagus keeps in an airtight container in the refrigerator for up to 2 months.

RIGHT: *Sweet-and-Sour
Pickled Asparagus, Asian-Spiced
Pickled Carrots (page 33), and
Dilled Green Beans (page 32)*

Tomato, Cucumber, & Mozzarella Skewers

MAKES 8 SKEWERS

One of the classic Italian starter salads is tomato and mozzarella with fresh basil leaves. Well, this is that salad on a stick. It's portable, and there's no need for a knife and fork. Choose great-quality tomatoes; even if they are a little more expensive, they will make the dish really vibrant. When you use good ingredients, they do the work for you—food is delicious without much effort required on your part. (And just take a moment to appreciate what the farmers have done for you!) You can easily double, triple, or halve this recipe depending on how many people you're feeding. I usually plan on serving three or four skewers per person as a snack.

8 (¼-inch-thick) slices seedless (English) cucumber, cut into quarters (triangles)

8 red grape tomatoes, halved if large

8 yellow pear tomatoes

8 bocconcini (small mozzarella balls)

2 tablespoons pesto (store-bought, or see page 131)

1 tablespoon extra-virgin olive oil

Freshly ground black pepper

On each of 8 bamboo skewers, thread a piece of cucumber, then a red tomato, then a piece of cucumber, then a mozzarella ball, then a piece of cucumber, then a yellow tomato, and finally a last piece of cucumber. Place the finished skewers on a serving plate. In a small bowl, combine the pesto with the olive oil to thin the pesto slightly and make it pourable. Drizzle the pesto over the skewers and grind a little pepper over them. Serve immediately or refrigerate in an airtight container for up to 1 day before serving.

PACK IT TO GO WITH:
Five-Bean Soup (page 101)

EAT IT AT HOME WITH:
Asparagus Risotto with Chives (page 124)

MAKE IT A PARTY WITH:
Gemelli with Peas and Pancetta (page 135)

Dates with Goat Cheese

MAKES 12 PIECES

I love pairing salty foods and sweet foods, and fruit with cheese is one of my favorite ways to do it. Here's a recipe for that winning combination. It's quick to make and portable too.

6 tablespoons goat cheese

1/8 teaspoon freshly ground black pepper

1/4 teaspoon snipped fresh chives

12 dates, pitted

PACK IT TO GO WITH:
Roasted Beets and Carrots with Orange (page 182)

EAT IT AT HOME WITH:
Grilled Muenster Cheese and Roasted Vegetable Sammie (page 82)

MAKE IT A PARTY WITH:
Teriyaki Chicken Salad (page 174) and Pumpkin Bread (page 60)

In a small bowl, combine the goat cheese, pepper, and chives and mix with a wooden spoon to make a smooth paste. Split the dates in half with a sharp knife and spread them open. Place a spoonful of the goat cheese filling inside each of the dates, then close the date over the goat cheese, leaving a small opening so the goat cheese mixture is visible. Serve immediately or store in an airtight container in the refrigerator until ready to serve. You can make these up to 2 days in advance and serve them chilled or at room temperature.

Homemade Banana Chips

MAKES ABOUT 2 CUPS

If one of my kids loves a certain store-bought snack food, I always try to figure out how to make my own version. My daughter Ella loves banana chips. She takes them to school for her morning snack, and they are her favorite grab-and-go snack for karate, long car rides, and picnics. I like making them myself, partly to save money, and partly so I know that no chemicals have been used to prepare them. Fruit chips make such a great lunch item because they keep better than many fresh fruits, can be eaten just a few pieces at a time, are packed with energy and vitamins but usually have almost no fat, pack well, and can easily be shared.

2 bananas, peeled and sliced into
⅛-inch-thick rounds

Heat the oven to 200 degrees. Grease a baking sheet with butter or canola oil, or line it with a Silpat mat.

Place the banana slices in a single layer on the prepared baking sheet and bake for 2 to 3 hours, until the chips feel almost dry and crisp. (They will dry out a little more as they cool.) Turn off the oven and let the chips cool in the oven for 1 hour with the door closed. The banana chips keep in a resealable bag at room temperature for up to 1 week.

PACK IT TO GO WITH:
a PB&J sandwich (page 77)

EAT IT AT HOME WITH:
ricotta and a drizzle of honey

MAKE IT A (DESSERT!) PARTY WITH:
vanilla ice cream, hot fudge, whipped cream, and toasted almonds (see Note, page 26)

Cheesy Focaccia Sticks

MAKES 12 PIECES

The idea for this recipe came from Connie Cinnamon (yes, that's her real name), a volunteer who worked with me in the kitchen at Elawa Farm, an organic farm in Lake Forest, Illinois. When I was working at the farm, I made focaccia weekly, and when we had leftovers, this is what we'd make. They are great as crunchy snacks, dippers for soup, or a nice side for a substantial salad. You don't have to make your own focaccia—if you purchase it, eat some of it fresh, and reserve the remainder to turn into focaccia sticks a day or two later.

1 to 1½ cups freshly grated Parmesan
½ teaspoon freshly ground black pepper

One 6x9-inch piece stale focaccia
⅓ to ½ cup extra-virgin olive oil

PACK IT TO GO WITH:
marinara sauce, for dipping

EAT IT AT HOME WITH:
*Vita's Pasta a Picchi Pacchi
(page 128)*

MAKE IT A PARTY WITH:
*Sausage and Escarole with
White Beans (page 156)*

Heat the oven to 400 degrees.

Spread the Parmesan out on a small tray and mix in the pepper. Using a serrated knife, cut the stale focaccia into ¾-inch-wide strips. Brush them lightly with olive oil on all sides, then dip each side in the Parmesan mixture. Place the focaccia strips on a baking sheet and toast them in the oven until light golden brown, 10 to 15 minutes, turning the sticks over once during cooking to help them brown evenly. Let cool completely on the pan. Store the focaccia sticks in a resealable bag at room temperature for up to 5 days.

Salsas, Spreads, & Such

Mango-Tomato Chutney

Simmered Tomato Salsa

Bell Pepper & Blistered Corn Salsa

Salsa Verde

Roasted Eggplant Spread

Gale's Guacamole

Hummus

Horseradish Sour Cream

Greek Potato-Garlic Schmear

Pea & Garlic Dip

Herbed Yogurt Dip

Apple Butter

Mango-Tomato Chutney

MAKES ABOUT 3 CUPS

This deliciously easy chutney is a wonderful way to add intense sweet-spicy-tart flavor to so many things. It's great spread on turkey sandwiches, dolloped on crackers and cheese, or served with cold meats. If this is more chutney than you think you can use in a month, halving the recipe works beautifully.

2 pounds plum tomatoes, seeded and chopped

2 medium mangoes, peeled, pit removed, and chopped

2 serrano peppers, minced

2 tablespoons grated lemon zest (from 2 to 3 lemons)

1½ cups sugar

1½ cups packed light brown sugar

6 tablespoons cider vinegar

2 teaspoons salt

¼ teaspoon freshly ground black pepper

⅛ teaspoon ground ginger

1 pinch ground cloves

1 pinch ground nutmeg

1 tablespoon chopped fresh cilantro

PACK IT TO GO WITH:
rolled turkey slices

EAT IT AT HOME WITH:
*a grilled cheese sandwich
(page 81)*

MAKE IT A PARTY WITH:
*Roasted Chicken (page 171)
and Garden Vegetable Coleslaw
(page 185)*

In a medium stainless steel saucepan, combine the tomatoes, mangoes, serrano peppers, and lemon zest. Stir in the sugar, brown sugar, vinegar, salt, pepper, ginger, cloves, nutmeg, and ½ cup water and simmer, uncovered, stirring frequently, for 1 hour. Let cool completely, then stir in the cilantro. The chutney keeps in an airtight container in the refrigerator for up to 1 month.

Simmered Tomato Salsa

MAKES 1½ CUPS

This is my favorite recipe for cooked tomato salsa. My son's girlfriend taught me how to make it. She learned it from her mother, who is from Mexico. Cooking the tomatoes for this salsa intensifies and sweetens their flavor, and pureeing the salsa creates a finer texture that works beautifully as a dip for chips and in enchiladas.

5 plum tomatoes

1 jalapeño, stemmed and quartered

1 clove garlic

1 tablespoon extra-virgin olive oil

Salt

6 fresh cilantro leaves, chopped

Remove the stem ends of the tomatoes and cut them in half lengthwise. Place the tomatoes and jalapeño in a saucepan with 1 tablespoon water and simmer over medium heat until they are soft and broken down a bit, 15 to 20 minutes.

Pour the mixture into a blender, scraping the pan well, add the garlic, and puree until smooth and well combined. In the same saucepan, heat the olive oil over medium heat until it is hot. Add the tomato-jalapeño puree and cook for 15 to 20 minutes to reduce and thicken it and to cook the garlic. Turn off the heat and let the salsa cool for 1 minute, then season with salt to taste. Set aside to cool completely.

Once the salsa has fully cooled, add the cilantro. Transfer the salsa to a bowl, cover it, and chill for 30 minutes. Serve the salsa with dippers like tortilla chips or vegetable sticks. The salsa keeps in an airtight container in the refrigerator for up to 1 week.

PACK IT TO GO WITH:
Cumin-Spiced Pita Chips (page 30) or corn chips

EAT IT AT HOME WITH:
Simple Chicken Burritos (page 148)

MAKE IT A PARTY WITH:
Spanish Tortilla (page 153) and Simple Green Salad (page 180)

Bell Pepper & Blistered Corn Salsa

MAKES 2 CUPS

This summery salsa is chunky and brightly colored, with bursts of red, green, and yellow. It's a great topping for chicken or fish, and I love it over cheesy scrambled eggs or with chips or jicama sticks for dipping.

2 ears corn (or 2 cups frozen roasted corn)

1 red bell pepper, seeded and chopped

1 green bell pepper, seeded and chopped

2 tablespoons extra-virgin olive oil, plus more for brushing

1 clove garlic, minced

1 tablespoon freshly squeezed lime juice

2 teaspoons chopped fresh flat-leaf parsley

2 teaspoons chopped fresh cilantro

Salt and freshly ground black pepper

PACK IT TO GO WITH:
celery sticks and bagel chips

EAT IT AT HOME WITH:
canned tuna and toasted baguette slices

MAKE IT A PARTY WITH:
Poached Chicken Breasts (page 172) and Roasted Cauliflower (page 187)

Heat your grill on medium. Brush the corn with olive oil. Grill the corn on all sides, turning as needed, until it browns slightly. Let cool for 5 minutes, then stand each ear of corn on its end in a bowl and use a sharp knife to cut the kernels off.

In a sauté pan, heat the olive oil over medium heat. Add the red and green bell peppers and cook, stirring, until tender, about 5 minutes. Add the garlic and cook for 30 seconds more. Pour the bell peppers and garlic into the bowl with the corn. Add the lime juice, parsley, and cilantro and mix, then taste and season with salt and pepper as needed. The salsa keeps in an airtight container in the refrigerator for up to 4 days.

RIGHT: *Bell Pepper & Blistered Corn Salsa and Salsa Verde (page 48)*

Salsa Verde

MAKES ABOUT 1½ CUPS

This versatile green salsa is a delicious dip for tortilla chips, pita chips (like the Cumin-Spiced Pita Chips on page 30), or cut veggies. You can also spoon it over chicken and rice to add a little kick to a simple meal, or over avocado slices for a memorable salad.

5 medium tomatillos

1 medium serrano chile

3 cloves garlic, unpeeled

Freshly squeezed juice of ½ lime

½ medium onion, chopped

10 sprigs fresh cilantro

1 teaspoon salt

PACK IT TO GO WITH:
Cumin-Spiced Pita Chips (page 30)

EAT IT AT HOME WITH:
pulled Roasted Chicken (page 171), warm tortillas, sour cream, and fresh ripe figs

MAKE IT A PARTY WITH:
chilled cooked shrimp, for dipping, and Three-Beet Salad with Snap Peas (page 181)

Peel the husks off the tomatillos and give the tomatillos a good washing to remove any stickiness. Using a small, sharp knife, score an X on the bottom of each tomatillo.

Move your oven rack to its highest position and preheat your broiler. Line a rimmed baking sheet with a layer of aluminum foil. Place the tomatillos, chile, and garlic on the baking sheet. Fold up the edges of the foil to make a rim that will catch any juices running from the tomatillos, then place the baking sheet under the broiler and broil until the skins of the tomatillos are charred, 4 to 5 minutes. Turn everything over and char the other side, 4 to 5 minutes more. Remove the baking sheet from the oven, being careful to reserve any juice in the foil tray. Place the tomatillos in the bowl of a food processor. Stem and seed the chile and peel the garlic. Add the chile and garlic to the bowl of the food processor along with the lime juice, onion, cilantro, and salt, and pulse until the ingredients are finely chopped and mixed well. The salsa keeps in an airtight container in the refrigerator for up to 1 week.

Roasted Eggplant Spread

MAKES 2 CUPS

Eggplant is one of those vegetables that some people just aren't sure how to tackle. In fact, it's not even a vegetable. It's a fruit—a berry, technically. Eggplants are simple and fun to cook with, and you can roast them to develop a soft, almost buttery texture that's great for mashing into a dip or spread. Large eggplants tend to be a little bitter, but salting them before cooking draws out some of the bitter liquid and improves their flavor. (With smaller eggplants, such as Japanese or baby eggplants, you can skip the salting step.)

1 large eggplant

$3/4$ teaspoon salt

1 small onion, sliced

1 clove garlic, sliced

$1/2$ teaspoon dried thyme, or 2 sprigs fresh thyme

$1/4$ teaspoon dried rosemary, or 1 sprig fresh rosemary

2 tablespoons extra-virgin olive oil

1 tablespoon freshly squeezed lemon juice

1 tablespoon fresh flat-leaf parsley leaves

Salt and freshly ground black pepper

Cut the eggplant in half and use a sharp knife to cut a deep crosshatch pattern into the cut side of each half, being careful not to cut through the skin. Spread the segments apart a bit and sprinkle half the salt over each half of the eggplant. Set aside on a plate for 30 minutes, then lightly squeeze the eggplant halves in your hands to force out the bitter water; discard the water.

Heat the oven to 400 degrees.

Scatter the onion, garlic, thyme, and rosemary on a rimmed baking sheet, then drizzle them with the olive oil and place the eggplant halves, cut side down, on top. Roast for about 30 minutes, until the eggplant looks deflated. Let cool on the pan for 10 minutes. Reserve the onion, garlic, and herbs and any juice the eggplant left on the baking sheet.

Scoop the soft eggplant flesh into the bowl of a food processor, discarding the skin. Add any juices from the baking sheet, the onion, garlic, herbs, lemon juice, parsley, and a couple grinds of pepper, then pulse to chop everything up into a spread. Taste for seasoning and add salt and more pepper if needed. Transfer the spread to a bowl, cover, and chill for 30 minutes. Serve with pita bread, crackers, or vegetables for dipping. The spread keeps in an airtight container in the refrigerator for up to 4 days.

PACK IT TO GO WITH:
Cheesy Focaccia Sticks (page 40)

EAT IT AT HOME WITH:
cold lamb chops

MAKE IT A PARTY: *spread it on horizontally sliced white bread (ask your local bakery to do it) with the crusts cut off, then roll up the bread and slice to make pinwheel sandwiches*

Gale's Guacamole

MAKES ABOUT 1 CUP

Guacamole is such a wonderful, simple, satisfying dip. Mine features a touch of cumin, jalapeños for heat (optional, of course), and a healthy squirt of lime juice, which brightens all the flavors and also helps keep the avocado from oxidizing and turning brown.

1 avocado, halved and pitted

1 small tomato, seeded and chopped

1 tablespoon minced onion

Freshly squeezed juice of ½ lime

1 jalapeño pepper, seeded and minced (optional; use less than a whole jalapeño, if you prefer)

6 fresh cilantro leaves, chopped

⅛ teaspoon ground cumin

⅛ teaspoon salt

2 grinds black pepper

PACK IT TO GO WITH:
carrot and cucumber sticks, for dipping

EAT IT AT HOME:
spread on a chicken sandwich

MAKE IT A PARTY:
place tortilla chips on a platter, top each chip with a piece of smoked salmon, spoon on a dollop of guacamole, then top with a cilantro leaf

Scoop the avocado flesh from the peel into a bowl. Mash the avocado with the back of a fork, then fold in the tomato, onion, lime juice, jalapeño, cilantro, cumin, salt, and pepper. The guacamole keeps in an airtight container in the refrigerator for up to 3 days; it may discolor somewhat during that time as the avocado oxidizes, but is still fine for eating.

Hummus

MAKES 2 CUPS

This delicious dip travels easily and keeps well, even if you're prepping it days ahead. I love the contrast of the sharp, fresh lemon juice with the mild chickpeas. And really, the hardest part of this recipe is getting your food processor out. The rest is a snap! Don't skip the tahini (sesame paste), which adds subtle flavor and improves the texture. Spring for a jar of tahini for the first batch and then you'll have it on hand the next dozen times you need it.

One 15-ounce can chickpeas, drained (reserve ¼ cup of the liquid)

3 tablespoons freshly squeezed lemon juice

1½ tablespoons tahini (sesame paste)

2 cloves garlic

½ teaspoon salt

2 tablespoons extra-virgin olive oil

Sprinkle of paprika

Combine the chickpeas, lemon juice, tahini, garlic, salt, and olive oil in the bowl of a food processor and process until very smooth. If you prefer a thinner consistency, add some of the reserved chickpea liquid and pulse to combine. Spoon the hummus into a serving bowl or plastic container and sprinkle with paprika. Serve or refrigerate immediately; the hummus can be served chilled or at room temperature and keeps in the refrigerator in an airtight container for up to 2 weeks.

PACK IT TO GO WITH:
carrots, bell pepper strips, and cucumber spears

EAT IT AT HOME WITH:
a drizzle of olive oil, a sprinkle of parsley, and Cumin-Spiced Pita Chips (page 30)

MAKE IT A PARTY:
spread on crostini, served with Wild Rice with Lentils and Spinach (page 123)

Horseradish Sour Cream

This is a great sauce to serve with smoked salmon or baked potatoes, or to spread on a steak or corned beef sandwich. The heat of the horseradish is mellowed by the sour cream, making this the perfect accompaniment for mild or salty foods.

1 cup sour cream

¼ cup mayonnaise

1 tablespoon Dijon mustard

¼ cup prepared grated white horseradish

1 tablespoon freshly squeezed lemon juice

1 tablespoon snipped fresh chives

½ teaspoon salt

¼ teaspoon freshly ground black pepper

PACK IT TO GO:
schmeared on a roast beef sandwich

EAT IT AT HOME WITH:
cold cooked shrimp, for dipping

MAKE IT A PARTY:
dolloped on sliced beef or pork tenderloin, served with Vinaigrette Potato Salad (page 188)

Combine the sour cream, mayonnaise, mustard, horseradish, lemon juice, chives, salt, and pepper in a small bowl. Cover and chill for at least 2 hours before serving, to marry the flavors. Serve chilled. This sauce keeps in an airtight container in the refrigerator for up to 2 weeks.

Greek Potato-Garlic Schmear

MAKES ABOUT 2 CUPS

I first had this "schmear" decades ago at a party in Rochester, New York. I don't remember who threw the party (a guy named Marty, I think), but this schmear was so delicious I never forgot it. Mashed potatoes are the perfect vehicle for showcasing the flavor of fresh garlic, because they mitigate some of its bite, or "heat," as chefs like to call it. This traditional Greek side dish is a delicious dip for vegetables or pita and is great alongside grilled lamb.

2 russet potatoes (about 1 pound), peeled and quartered

1 teaspoon salt

2 to 3 cloves garlic (depending on how garlicky you like things)

½ cup extra-virgin olive oil

2 tablespoons freshly squeezed lemon juice

Freshly ground black pepper

Place the potatoes in a medium pot, add enough water to cover them, and salt the water. Bring the water to a boil and cook until the potatoes are fork tender, 15 to 20 minutes.

Meanwhile, on a cutting board, sprinkle the garlic cloves with the salt and smash them with the side of a large, heavy knife, then very finely chop them.

Drain the potatoes, then place them in a bowl and mash them well, or process them through a ricer into a bowl. (Don't use a food processor here or the potatoes will become gummy.) Stir in the garlic, olive oil, lemon juice, and pepper. The schmear keeps in an airtight container in the refrigerator for up to 1 week.

PACK IT TO GO WITH:
sliced baguette to schmear it on

EAT IT AT HOME WITH:
hollowed-out cucumber boats filled with it

MAKE IT A PARTY WITH:
pita triangles, celery sticks, carrot sticks, fennel sticks, and bell pepper strips, for dipping

Pea & Garlic Dip

MAKES ABOUT 3 CUPS

This is one of the fastest, easiest things I make, and it's addictive. It uses frozen peas (so you can prepare it year-round), a little salt, pepper, and garlic for flavor, and a bit of olive oil to make it smooth. It keeps for days, staying bright green all the while, and is great as a dip, crostini topper, or sandwich spread.

1 pound frozen peas, thawed
10 fresh mint leaves (optional)
2 medium cloves garlic
½ teaspoon salt, plus more as needed

⅛ teaspoon freshly ground black pepper, plus more as needed
6 tablespoons extra-virgin olive oil

Place the peas, mint (if using), garlic, salt, pepper, and olive oil in a food processor and process until well blended and relatively smooth. (The mixture will retain some texture, but make it as smooth as possible.) Taste and season with additional salt and pepper as needed. Serve immediately or transfer to a bowl, cover, and chill until ready to serve. The dip keeps in an airtight container in the refrigerator for up to 4 days.

PACK IT TO GO WITH:
carrot sticks

EAT IT AT HOME WITH:
flatbread, or spread on a turkey sandwich

MAKE IT A PARTY:
spread it on crostini—and top it with a piece of smoked salmon, small chilled cooked shrimp, or a thin slice of beef tenderloin with coarse salt, if you wish—for a pretty lunchtime appetizer

Herbed Yogurt Dip

MAKES 2½ CUPS

This is a light, creamy dip that's low in fat but high in flavor. All the herbs give it a garden-fresh taste, which I love. My favorite way to eat this dip is with jicama sticks—they have satisfying crunch, but no fat or sodium. Just pack the dip in a container with a lid, put the jicama sticks in a small resealable bag, and go!

2 cups Greek yogurt

½ cup cottage cheese

1 teaspoon freshly squeezed lemon juice

1 scallion, sliced

¼ cup loosely packed flat-leaf parsley leaves

1 clove garlic

1 tablespoon snipped fresh chives

½ teaspoon dried dill

½ teaspoon salt

½ teaspoon freshly ground black pepper

PACK IT TO GO WITH:
jicama sticks

EAT IT AT HOME WITH:
seedless (English) cucumber slices and a wedge of Spanish Tortilla (page 153)

MAKE IT A PARTY WITH:
Chicken Drumsticks with Chili Sauce (page 150) and fresh, trimmed green beans and snap peas

Combine the yogurt, cottage cheese, lemon juice, scallion, parsley, garlic, chives, dill, salt, and pepper in the bowl of a food processor and process until the ingredients are well combined and the garlic is finely chopped. Serve immediately, or transfer to a bowl, cover, and chill until ready to serve. The dip keeps in an airtight container in the refrigerator for up to 3 days.

Apple Butter

MAKES ABOUT 2 CUPS

Even though this is called "butter," there's no butter, or fat, in it! It's just apples (use whichever kind you like), brown sugar, and spices. My family adores it—we keep it in the house to spread on toast or crumpets and to use in PB&J sandwiches, as well as in the Apple Pie Pops on page 229. And in moments of utter decadence, it has even landed on oatmeal cookies.

1½ pounds apples, peeled, cored, and cut into ½-inch chunks

½ cup packed light brown sugar

½ teaspoon ground cinnamon

¼ teaspoon ground ginger

Place the apples in a medium heavy-bottomed pot. Cook over low heat, uncovered, stirring occasionally, for 1½ hours. The apples will break down as they cook. Add the brown sugar, cinnamon, and ginger and stir to combine. Continue cooking, stirring occasionally, until very thick, about 30 minutes more.

To test for doneness, place a spoonful of the mixture on a white plate and let it sit for 20 seconds. If a ring of liquid forms around the apples, there is still too much liquid in the mixture; continue to cook the apples for a few minutes and test again until no ring forms. The apple butter keeps in an airtight container in the refrigerator for up to 2 months.

PACK IT TO GO WITH:
slices of Pumpkin Bread (page 60) and almond butter

EAT IT AT HOME:
stirred into yogurt with Gale's Trail Mix (page 26)

MAKE IT A PARTY:
spread on toasted peanut butter sandwiches with tall glasses of milk

Quick Breads

Pumpkin Bread

Apple Spice Muffins

Parmesan–Black Pepper Corn Muffins

Chipotle Cheddar Biscuits

Ginger Peach Muffins

Honey Mustard Pretzel Rolls

Savory Scallion & Bacon Scones

Buttermilk Oatmeal Bran Muffins

Pumpkin Bread

MAKES 1 LOAF

This is one of my favorite recipes to make with my kids because it's a stir-it-yourself deal. No mixer needed, except your kids and their wooden spoons! I add a little whole wheat flour for nutrition and for its nutty, toasty flavor. If you're looking for something to do with the buttermilk that's left in the carton after you use the half cup this recipe calls for, I suggest the Parmesan–Black Pepper Corn Muffins on page 62, the Chipotle Cheddar Biscuits on page 65, or the buttermilk pancakes on page 80 of my brunch cookbook, Gale Gand's Brunch! Nobody will be unhappy about that!

3 large eggs

1 cup sugar

½ cup canola oil

One 15-ounce can pumpkin puree (not pumpkin pie filling)

½ cup light molasses

½ cup buttermilk

2 cups all-purpose flour

¾ cup whole wheat flour

1 teaspoon ground cinnamon

½ teaspoon ground ginger

½ teaspoon ground nutmeg

1 pinch ground cloves

1½ teaspoons baking soda

1 teaspoon salt

PACK IT TO GO WITH:
applesauce and yogurt

EAT IT AT HOME WITH:
a schmear of cream cheese

MAKE IT A PARTY WITH:
Butternut Squash and Apple Soup (page 104) and Simple Green Salad (page 180) topped with Chicken Salad with Dried Cranberries (page 176)

Heat the oven to 350 degrees. Line a standard loaf pan with parchment paper.

In a medium bowl, whisk the eggs well for about 1 minute, then use a wooden spoon to stir in the sugar and the oil. Add the pumpkin, molasses, and buttermilk and mix well. In a separate bowl, combine the all-purpose flour, whole wheat flour, cinnamon, ginger, nutmeg, cloves, baking soda, and salt and stir until blended well.

Add the dry ingredients to the wet ingredients and stir until just blended; do not overmix. Spoon the batter into the prepared loaf pan. Bake for 40 to 45 minutes, until the bread has risen and is firm to the touch in the center. Let cool completely in the pan, set on a wire rack. When cool, invert the loaf into your hand and place it on a cutting board to slice and serve. The bread keeps, wrapped tightly in plastic wrap, in the refrigerator for up to 2 weeks, or frozen in a resealable freezer bag for up to 1 month.

Apple Spice Muffins

MAKES 24 MUFFINS

At the end of the fall, I tend to inherit bushels of questionable apples—the ones no one else wants because they are a little bruised and bumpy—from the various farmers I work with. I can't bear to throw them out, so what to do with them? I make apple butter—lots of apple butter. In my house we spread it on toast, scones, and crumpets and dip chicken into it, and my husband even eats it with fried eggs (don't ask). I also use it in hand pies (see page 226) and these easy, delicious muffins.

3 large eggs

1 cup sugar

½ cup canola oil

2 cups Apple Butter (page 57)

½ cup mild light molasses

½ cup buttermilk

2¾ cups all-purpose flour

2 teaspoons pumpkin pie spice (or 1¼ teaspoon cinnamon, ½ teaspoon ginger, and ¼ teaspoon nutmeg)

1½ teaspoons baking soda

1 teaspoon salt

Heat the oven to 350 degrees. Line a standard muffin tin with paper liners.

In a large bowl, whisk the eggs well, then use a wooden spoon to stir in the sugar and the oil. Add the apple butter, molasses, and buttermilk and stir well. In a separate bowl, mix together the flour, pumpkin pie spice, baking soda, and salt. Add the dry ingredients to the wet ingredients and stir just until blended. With a spoon, fill the muffin cups two-thirds full with the batter. Bake for about 20 minutes, until the muffins are firm to the touch in the center. The muffins will keep in an airtight container at room temperature for up to 4 days, or in the freezer, wrapped tightly in plastic, for up to 1 month.

PACK IT TO GO WITH:
cream cheese, for schmearing

EAT IT AT HOME WITH:
Roasted Chicken (page 171) and Roasted Pumpkin with Scallion, Rosemary, and Raisins (page 197)

MAKE IT A PARTY WITH:
Chicken Salad with Dried Cranberries, Fennel, and Toasted Almonds (page 176) and Iced Tea (page 245) with Vanilla Syrup (page 245)

Parmesan–Black Pepper Corn Muffins

MAKES 12 MUFFINS

Parmesan and black pepper is one of my favorite flavor combinations. I use it in scrambled eggs, biscuits, and pasta dough, and even over popcorn (see page 22). In a way, it's similar to adding salt and pepper to a dish, because Parmesan provides some of the saltiness needed for flavor in recipes. But Parmesan also has a unique savory flavor that takes things up a notch. Serve these muffins with vegetable chili, a bowl of soup, or a salad for a satisfying meal.

1 cup yellow cornmeal

1 cup all-purpose flour

4 teaspoons baking powder

½ teaspoon salt

¾ cup freshly grated Parmesan cheese

1 teaspoon freshly ground black pepper

1 large egg

1¼ cups buttermilk

⅓ cup honey (preferably local)

4 tablespoons unsalted butter, melted

PACK IT TO GO WITH:
Chicken Drumsticks with Chili Sauce (page 150)

EAT IT AT HOME WITH:
Four-Bean Vegetable Chili (page 102)

MAKE IT A PARTY WITH:
Gale's Gazpacho (page 97) and Smoked Salmon Caesar Salad (page 164)

Heat the oven to 425 degrees. Line a standard muffin tin with paper liners.

In a medium bowl, stir together the cornmeal, flour, baking powder, salt, Parmesan, and pepper. In another small bowl, beat the egg with a fork, then stir in the buttermilk, honey, and melted butter. Pour the egg mixture into the cornmeal mixture and stir until just combined; do not overmix. Fill the muffin cups two-thirds full, and bake for 15 to 20 minutes, until the muffins have risen and are firm to the touch in the center. Let cool for about 10 minutes, then remove the muffins from the pan and serve while they are still warm, or let them cool completely and store them in an airtight container at room temperature for up to 2 days or freeze them in a resealable freezer bag for up to 1 month.

Chipotle Cheddar Biscuits

MAKES ABOUT TWELVE 2-INCH BISCUITS

I've made all kinds of biscuits—and lots of them—over the years: tiny black pepper–Parmesan biscuits at Tru, big ol' baking powder biscuits at Elawa Farm, and spoon biscuits at home for chicken and dumplings. I love them all. These chipotle cheddar biscuits are my current favorites. They're cheesy with a kick of chipotle, and they're delicious with soup.

2¼ cups all-purpose flour, plus more for your work surface

4 teaspoons baking powder

1½ teaspoons salt

⅛ teaspoon freshly ground black pepper

1 tablespoon plus 1 teaspoon sugar

2 teaspoons smoked or regular paprika

1 teaspoon ground chipotle

1 cup grated sharp cheddar cheese

2 tablespoons chopped fresh scallions

½ cup (1 stick) cold unsalted butter, cut into ½-inch cubes

1 cup buttermilk

Heat the oven to 400 degrees. Line a baking sheet with parchment paper.

In the bowl of a stand mixer fitted with the paddle attachment, combine the flour, baking powder, salt, pepper, sugar, paprika, chipotle, ½ cup of the cheddar, and the scallions. Mix on low speed for 30 seconds to combine and blend in the spices. Add the butter and continue to mix on low speed to break down the butter, mixing just until the butter pieces are the size of peas. Add the buttermilk and mix until just combined. Turn the dough onto a floured work surface and knead it slightly to bring it together, if necessary. Roll out the dough to ¾ inch thick and cut out 2-inch-diameter circles with a cookie or biscuit cutter. Place the circles on the lined baking sheet. Press the dough scraps together, roll them out again, and cut out as many biscuits as you can. Repeat until you've used all the dough. Evenly distribute the remaining ½ cup cheddar over the tops of the biscuits.

Bake for 12 to 15 minutes, until the biscuits are puffed up and golden brown on top. The biscuits keep in an airtight container for up to 1 day at room temperature or up to 4 days in the refrigerator. If refrigerating, reheat them in a 350-degree toaster oven for about 5 minutes before serving.

PACK IT TO GO WITH: *sliced ham and spicy brown mustard*

EAT IT AT HOME WITH: *Corn Chowder (page 105)*

MAKE IT A PARTY WITH: *Cobb Salad (page 168) and Blackberry Rice Pudding (page 225)*

Ginger Peach Muffins

MAKES 12 MUFFINS

One of my jobs (and I have about ten!) has been working as the chef-in-residence at Elawa Farm, a historic farm outside of Chicago. This is hands-down the favorite muffin of the customers at the farm's market. In July and August, peaches are in season, so I load up the batter with them, but when peach season ends I switch to plums or pears or whatever looks good at the market—same quantity, just different fruit.

1 large egg

½ cup plus 2 tablespoons sugar

6 tablespoons unsalted butter, melted

½ cup buttermilk

1½ cups all-purpose flour

1½ teaspoons baking powder

½ teaspoon ground ginger

½ teaspoon salt

1 cup unpeeled chopped ripe peaches (1 to 2 peaches, depending on size)

Sugar in the Raw or other coarse sugar, for sprinkling

PACK IT TO GO WITH:
Summer Berries in Hibiscus Syrup (page 206) and Greek yogurt

EAT IT AT HOME WITH:
scrambled eggs with snipped chives

MAKE IT A PARTY WITH:
Butternut Squash and Apple Soup (page 104) and Israeli Couscous with Cranberries and Toasted Pecans (page 119)

Heat the oven to 375 degrees. Line a standard muffin tin with paper liners.

In a medium bowl, whisk together the egg and sugar, then whisk in the melted butter, followed by the buttermilk. In a large bowl, stir together the flour, baking powder, ginger, and salt. Pour the egg mixture over the flour mixture and fold together gently with a rubber spatula until almost mixed, but stopping while bits of flour are still visible; do not overmix. Add the peaches and fold the batter a few more times to mix them in. Using an ice cream scoop, scoop the batter into the paper liners, filling them about three-quarters full. Sprinkle the batter well with Sugar in the Raw or another coarse sugar. Bake for 25 to 30 minutes, until golden brown and firm to the touch in the center. Let the muffins cool in the pan for 10 minutes, then lift them out of the pan and transfer them to a wire rack to cool completely. The muffins will keep in an airtight container at room temperature for 2 days, or in a freezer bag in the freezer for up to 1 month.

Honey Mustard Pretzel Rolls

MAKES TEN 3-INCH ROLLS

These little rolls (which technically aren't a quick bread because they contain yeast, but they require no proofing time) make great bread for petite sandwiches. Slice them open and pile them with prosciutto and cheese or egg salad, or serve them with soup for a nice little meal. You don't need mustard; it's in the bread! Boiling the rolls gives them a chewy exterior like a bagel, and the baking soda in the water gives them that shiny surface.

½ cup baking soda

1 cup plus 2 tablespoons warm water

1 package dry yeast

⅓ cup honey

2 teaspoons dry mustard powder

5 cups all-purpose flour, plus more for your work surface

Sea salt, for sprinkling

Heat the oven to 450 degrees. Butter 2 baking sheets.

Bring 2 quarts of water and the baking soda to a boil in a large pot.

In the bowl of a stand mixer, whisk 2 tablespoons warm water with the yeast until the yeast is completely dissolved. Whisk in the remaining 1 cup warm water and the honey. Place the bowl on the mixer and fit the mixer with the dough hook. Add the mustard powder and begin mixing on low speed. Gradually add the flour and continue mixing until the dough forms a ball. Turn the dough out onto a floured work surface and knead until smooth. (Use enough flour on your work surface so the dough is not sticky.)

Cut the dough into egg-size pieces, then roll the pieces into 1-inch-thick oblong rolls. Drop the pieces a few at a time into the boiling water. Let them cook for 30 seconds, then fish them out with a slotted spoon and place them on the prepared baking sheets. Repeat with the remaining dough. Sprinkle the boiled rolls with sea salt, then bake for 10 to 12 minutes, until golden brown. Let the rolls cool completely on the baking sheets, then store them in an airtight container at room temperature for up to 2 days.

PACK IT TO GO WITH:
sliced prosciutto and fresh mozzarella balls

EAT IT AT HOME:
stuffed with Gale's Egg Salad (page 87)

MAKE IT A PARTY WITH:
Potato Leek Soup (page 106) and Roasted Asparagus with Walnuts and Goat Cheese (page 196)

Savory Scallion & Bacon Scones

MAKES 10 SCONES

I like fruited scones for breakfast and savory scones for lunch. This is the perfect lunchtime scone—try it with soup or a salad, or split it in half to make a sandwich. (I like it with turkey and cheddar, or chicken salad.) If you're a believer in the "Everything's Better with Bacon" mantra, you'll love this one. And for the nonbelievers, these scones are also very good without the bacon.

2 cups all-purpose flour

1 teaspoon salt

½ teaspoon freshly ground black pepper

1 tablespoon baking powder

½ cup chopped scallions

½ cup crumbled cooked bacon (from 4 to 6 slices)

¾ cup (1½ sticks) unsalted butter, cut into ½-inch cubes

2 large eggs

½ cup sour cream

PACK IT TO GO WITH:
tomato slices and Blue Cheese Vinaigrette (page 169)

EAT IT AT HOME WITH:
Wild Rice with Lentils and Spinach (page 123)

MAKE IT A PARTY WITH:
Smoked Salmon Caesar (page 164) and Blueberry Hand Pies (page 226)

Heat the oven to 400 degrees. Line a baking sheet with parchment paper.

In the bowl of a stand mixer fitted with the paddle attachment, place the flour, salt, pepper, baking powder, scallions, and bacon and mix on low to combine. Add the butter and mix until the pieces of butter are pea-size. In a small bowl, whisk the eggs and sour cream together with a fork to combine. Add the egg mixture to the flour mixture and mix until just moistened.

Using a large ice cream scoop, scoop the batter onto the parchment-lined baking sheet, leaving about 1½ inches between the scones so they have room to expand during baking. Bake for 20 to 25 minutes, until light golden brown. Let cool completely on the pan. The scones will keep at room temperature in an airtight container or resealable bag for up to 3 days, or frozen in a freezer bag for up to 1 month. If you freeze them, defrost them at room temperature for 2 hours, then warm them in the oven or toaster oven at 350 degrees before serving.

Buttermilk Oatmeal Bran Muffins

MAKES 12 MUFFINS

I used to own a bakery-café called Vanilla Bean Bakery, where we made artisanal breads, croissants, cakes, muffins, scones, soup, sandwiches, and cookies. I opened it the year my son, Gio, was born, and I used to bring him to work with me at midnight. He would sleep in his carrier on the wooden workbench while I made bread all night. My theory was that I was helping him develop his olfactory memory, smelling all that bread baking while he slept, though I always worried a bit that the smell of baking bread might put him to sleep in his adult life. (He's seventeen now and, so far, no bread-induced narcolepsy!) This was one of the popular muffins from that bakery. Letting the oats and bran soak beforehand makes for a more tender texture.

2 cups rolled oats (not quick-cooking), plus more for sprinkling

½ cup bran

2 cups buttermilk

1½ cups all-purpose flour

1½ teaspoons baking powder

1½ teaspoons baking soda

1 teaspoon salt

1 teaspoon ground cinnamon

2 large eggs

¾ cup packed light brown sugar

¾ cup (1½ sticks) unsalted butter, melted

⅔ cup currants or raisins

In a large bowl, combine the oats, bran, and buttermilk and let sit at room temperature, stirring occasionally, for 30 minutes.

Heat the oven to 375 degrees. Line a standard muffin tin with paper liners.

In a bowl, stir together the flour, baking powder, baking soda, salt, and cinnamon.

Add the eggs to the oat mixture and mix with a wooden spoon until well combined. Add the brown sugar and butter and mix until thoroughly incorporated. Gradually add the flour mixture and mix until just combined, leaving the batter a bit lumpy. Fold in the currants.

Use a large spoon or an ice cream scoop to fill the muffin cups three-quarters full. Sprinkle with rolled oats. Bake for 20 to 25 minutes, until the muffins are risen and golden brown, and a toothpick inserted in the center comes out clean (a few crumbs are okay). Let cool for at least 10 minutes in the pan. Let cool completely before storing in an airtight container at room temperature for up to 3 days or frozen in a freezer bag for up to 1 month.

PACK IT TO GO WITH:
Butternut Squash and Apple Soup (page 104)

EAT IT AT HOME WITH:
Tropical Fruit Salad (page 204)

MAKE IT A PARTY WITH:
Barley with Wild Mushrooms, Broccoli, and Scallions (page 118) and Simple Green Salad (page 180)

Sammies

Grilled Skirt Steak with Arugula

Turkey Reuben

Turkey with Mango-Tomato Chutney

PB&J 101

Ham & Provolone with Giardiniera

Cuban Sandwich

Grilled Cheese 101

Classic Lobster Roll

Egg Salad 101

Bertha's Tuna Salad

Chicken Salad Sliders

Fried Chicken & Waffle Sandwiches

Grilled Skirt Steak with Arugula

MAKES 2 SANDWICHES

Bistecca alla Fiorentina *is a traditional Italian dish served all over Florence, and I think it's one of the most wonderful things ever. It's a bed of arugula topped with slices of garlicky grilled steak, shards of shaved Parmesan, and a squeeze of tart fresh lemon juice. Here it is in a form that requires no silverware. Ask your butcher to "jacquard" your steak for you. That's a form of tenderizing done with a tool that looks like a bed of nails or fork tines; the tool pierces the flesh of the steak, breaking the tissue to allow flavor in.*

¼ cup extra-virgin olive oil, plus more for the buns

2 tablespoons balsamic vinegar

3 cloves garlic, minced

½ teaspoon freshly ground black pepper

1 skirt steak or skirt hanger (about 1 pound), cleaned, trimmed of fat, and jacquarded

½ to 1 teaspoon salt

2 ciabatta sandwich buns

2 cups arugula

Block Parmesan cheese, for shaving

Horseradish Sour Cream (page 52)

PACK IT TO GO WITH:
root vegetable chips

EAT IT AT HOME WITH:
Asian-Spiced Pickled Carrots (page 32)

MAKE IT A PARTY WITH:
Loaded Potato Salad (page 190) and Orange-Scented Chocolate Brownies (page 214)

Place the olive oil, vinegar, garlic, and pepper in a resealable bag and seal it. Massage the bag to combine the ingredients. Place the steak in the bag, reseal the bag, and tumble it to coat the steak in the marinade. Let the steak marinate for 30 minutes at room temperature or for up to 8 hours in the refrigerator.

Heat your grill on medium heat. Remove the steak from the bag, place it on a plate, and sprinkle the salt on both sides. When the grill is hot, grill the steak for 4 to 6 minutes per side (8 to 12 minutes total), depending on how thick the steak is and how rare or well done you like your steak. If you'd like, place the meat so the thinner parts are at the edge of the grill, away from the direct heat, so they don't overcook.

Slice the sandwich buns in half and brush the cut sides with olive oil. Place the buns, cut sides down, on the grill and toast for 2 to 3 minutes. Place each bun on a plate and mound half of the arugula on the bottom half of each bun.

Let the cooked steak rest for 5 minutes, then slice it against the grain. Place half the slices on top of the arugula on each bun. Top the steak slices with Parmesan shaved with a vegetable peeler. Spread horseradish sour cream liberally on the toasted side of the top half of the bun, place the top over the steak and Parmesan, and serve immediately.

Turkey Reuben

MAKES 1 SANDWICH

This is a cross between a mouthwatering grilled cheese and a classic Reuben. But it's lighter than you'd expect, because it's made with turkey instead of corned beef. If you have a panini press, fire it up for this sandwich. If not, pan toast it for delicious results.

2 teaspoons unsalted butter

2 pieces caraway rye bread

¼ pound sliced roasted turkey (about 4 slices)

½ cup sauerkraut

2 tablespoons Thousand Island dressing

3 slices Swiss cheese

PACK IT TO GO WITH:
pickles (page 32)

EAT IT AT HOME WITH:
slices of ripe pear

MAKE IT A PARTY WITH:
Matzo Ball Soup (page 109) and Big Chewy Chocolate Chip Cookies (page 210)

Butter one side of each of the rye bread slices. Place one slice, butter side down, in a nonstick frying pan and then build the sandwich on top of it, starting with the turkey, followed by the sauerkraut. Spread the dressing as evenly as possible over the sauerkraut, then top the dressing with the cheese.

Place the remaining buttered bread slice on top, butter side up, and turn the heat under the pan to medium. Toast the bread until golden brown, about 4 minutes after the pan warms up, then carefully flip the sandwich over with a spatula to toast the other side of the sandwich until golden brown, 3 to 4 minutes more. Remove the sandwich from the pan and place it on a cutting board to cool for 1 minute, then cut it in half and serve immediately.

Turkey with Mango-Tomato Chutney

MAKES 1 SANDWICH

My husband is crazy about turkey sandwiches with mango chutney. Chutney is one of the "must-have" items in our fridge. If we're getting low, a trip to the store is in order whether we need it immediately or not, because inevitably he'll have a craving. Turkey is so mild in flavor that it's the perfect backdrop for the strong and exotic flavors of chutney. My Mango-Tomato Chutney (page 44) is lovely in this sandwich, especially if you like a little kick from serrano peppers.

2 slices crusty sourdough bread

2 tablespoons mayonnaise

2 iceberg lettuce leaves

1 piece jarred roasted red pepper, cut into strips

2 tablespoons Mango-Tomato Chutney (page 44) or prepared mango chutney (such as Major Grey's)

½ avocado, peeled and sliced

¼ pound sliced roasted turkey (about 4 slices)

2 slices pepper Jack cheese

Spread one side of each piece of bread with the mayonnaise. On one slice of bread, layer the lettuce leaves and the pepper strips over the mayonnaise. Spread the chutney on next, then layer on the avocado slices. Place the turkey on top of the avocado, and finish with the cheese. Top the cheese with the other slice of bread, mayonnaise side down. Cut the sandwich in half diagonally and serve, or place in a resealable bag and chill until ready to eat, preferably within a few hours.

PACK IT TO GO WITH:
pineapple chunks

EAT IT AT HOME WITH:
an Apricot Lime Sparkler (page 248)

MAKE IT A PARTY WITH:
Vinaigrette Potato Salad (page 180) and Everything Cookies (page 212)

PB & J 101

The peanut butter and jelly sandwich is an American classic. And of course the PB&J combination has gone far beyond bread, into bread pudding, ice cream, and more, so it's obviously beloved. PB&J has synergy like nothing else. I think it's one of the best combinations of salty and sweet around.

My vegetarian brother lived on nothing but PB&J sandwiches for lunch for eight straight years, so my family got to know this classic combo very well. (His jelly of choice was crab apple, and for dinner he would have the same thing, but wrapped inside crêpes.)

For me, grape jelly or jam is the way to go, especially if you make your own, which I do (see opposite). My family and I picked Concord grapes one year in Michigan, and the jam I made from those grapes was stellar because the grapes themselves were so good. Every year I try to get some Concord grapes and re-create it, making plenty so I can give some to friends on my "nice" list when the holidays roll around.

The big questions you must ask yourself are: Chunky or smooth? Natural or processed? Jelly, jam, or preserves? White or whole grain bread? Should the bread be cold, warmed, or toasted? Crust cut off or left on? Peanut butter on both pieces of bread with the jelly sandwiched in between (my husband insists this is the only way to do it) or jelly on one piece of bread and peanut butter on the other?

If you're not sure where you stand on these questions, start with the classic recipe on the next page and then vary it based on your personal preferences. Then consider add-ons like sliced bananas, a drizzle of honey, ripe pear slices, Apple Butter (page 57), strips of cooked bacon, a sprinkle of raisins, green apple wedges, pineapple chunks, crushed cashews or almonds, dried cherries, or (dare I say it) Marshmallow Fluff.

Ultimate PB&J

MAKES 1 SANDWICH

¼ cup super-chunky peanut butter

2 slices oatmeal bread

2 tablespoons Concord Grape Jam (recipe below) or store-bought grape jam

Spread half the peanut butter on one side of each piece of bread. Spread the jam over the peanut butter on one piece of bread. Put the slices together to enclose the jelly. Cut the sandwich in half, corner to corner (making the sandwich easier to insert into your mouth than if you cut it in half straight down the middle). Eat!

Concord Grape Jam

MAKES ABOUT 4 HALF-PINT JARS

This is a great homemade treat to give as a gift! Or to keep for yourself, of course.

1½ pounds Concord grapes

3½ cups sugar

3 tablespoons powdered pectin

Place the grapes in a saucepan and bring them to a boil over medium-high heat to burst the skins, stirring occasionally. Once they've boiled, turn the heat off and let the grapes cool slightly. Break down the grape skins slightly by blending with a hand blender for about 30 seconds (you don't want to break down the seeds, though). Pour the fruit through a coarse sieve (I use a colander), using a rubber spatula to push the fruit through, straining out the seeds and large pieces of skin. You should end up with about 2 cups of strained fruit pulp.

Place the fruit pulp, sugar, and pectin in a large pot and stir to combine well. Bring the mixture to a full rolling boil over high heat and let boil for exactly 1 minute more. Turn off the heat, skim off any foam, and pour the hot jam into clean jars, leaving ¼ inch of headspace at the top of the jars. Put the lids on immediately and let cool completely at room temperature before serving or refrigerating. The jam will keep in jars in the refrigerator for up to 6 months.

Ham & Provolone with Giardiniera

MAKES 1 SANDWICH

My love affair with Tony's Sub Shop in Deerfield, Illinois, began when I was six (the year the shop opened) and has continued ever since. It was just a counter at the back of the Dairy Store, a narrow little store on the way to "Up Town," in Deerfield's town center. It's still around, but in a different location, because it became so popular that it needed more space. My favorite Tony's sandwich has always been the Ham and Provolone, with its yummy ham and cheese, bread lightly dressed with olive oil instead of mayo, shredded fresh lettuce, and a kick from the spicy giardiniera relish. This is the version I make at home.

One 8-inch sub roll, split horizontally

2 teaspoons extra-virgin olive oil

1 teaspoon giardiniera relish

½ teaspoon dried oregano

8 thin slices deli ham, folded to fit the bread

2 slices provolone cheese, folded to fit the bread

½ leaf romaine lettuce

1 piece jarred roasted red pepper, cut into 4 strips

PACK IT TO GO WITH:
cold Roasted Cauliflower (page 187)

EAT IT AT HOME WITH:
Garden Vegetable Coleslaw (page 185)

MAKE IT A PARTY WITH:
crudités and Pea and Garlic Dip (page 55)

Open the sub roll and drizzle the inside surfaces with the olive oil. Smear the giardiniera relish on one side and sprinkle the oregano on both sides. Layer the ham, cheese, and lettuce over the relish and top with the pepper strips. Close the roll and cut it in half crosswise on the diagonal. Serve immediately.

Cuban Sandwich

MAKES 1 SANDWICH

This is a Cuban variation on a ham and cheese sandwich. It was a favorite lunch of the workers in the cigar factories in Cuba, and then it became a hit in Miami, where some of the best Cuban sandwiches are now made. When my husband and I started dating, he used to make me tapes of songs about food. There were songs like "Strawberry Jam," "Black Coffee in Bed," and "Okra!," and then there was one by Barrence Whitfield about a Cuban sandwich. We loved the song, and we started eating Cuban sandwiches all over the place, looking for the most authentic ones. Here's the one we make at home. To make it you do need some kind of sandwich press, which is something I think every kitchen ought to have anyway!

One 6-inch sub roll, split horizontally

2 tablespoons yellow mustard

¼ pound sliced deli ham (about 4 slices)

¼ pound sliced roasted pork

3 slices Swiss or provolone cheese

Dill pickle slices

2 teaspoons unsalted butter

Open the sub roll. Spread the mustard on both of the cut sides, then layer on the ham, pork, and cheese, and top with enough pickle slices to completely cover the cheese. Close the roll. Butter the outside of the roll on both sides and grill the sandwich in a *plancha* (sandwich press) or a panini press (or in a skillet with a heated heavy iron pan pressed on top) until the cheese melts, 8 to 10 minutes. Cut the sandwich in half diagonally and serve immediately.

PACK IT TO GO WITH:
an orange

EAT IT AT HOME WITH:
Baked Kale Chips (page 20)

MAKE IT A PARTY WITH:
a salad of hearts of palm, tomato wedges, and avocado chunks with Mustard Vinaigrette (page 162), and Iced Tea (page 245) with Minted Iced Tea Cubes (page 247)

Grilled Cheese 101
(a.k.a. *The Big Meltdown*)

I thought a recipe for the quintessential grilled cheese sandwich would be the simplest to write for this book, but then I started thinking about the possibilities and the recipe got longer and longer. Now I'm thinking it might need its own book! At its most basic, a grilled cheese sandwich features some kind of cheese or cheeses between slices of buttered bread. (Make sure the butter is at room temperature when you spread it so it doesn't tear the bread.) The buttery sides of the sandwich are then cooked in a skillet or sauté pan, and the heat melts the cheese inside. You can add spreads and/or other ingredients to the inside of the sandwich.

My basic grilled cheese is so tasty that I get emails from other moms after playdates asking me for my recipe. It's not fancy, but here it is! And I encourage you to play around with this and try different kinds of bread, cheese, spreads, and add-ins from the lists on the next page.

Basic Grilled Cheese

MAKES 1 SANDWICH

2 teaspoons unsalted butter, at room
temperature

2 slices white bread

3 slices cheese (I like 2 slices American
and 1 slice Muenster)

Butter one side of each piece of bread. Place one slice in a sauté pan, butter side down, then cover it with 1 slice American cheese, 1 slice Muenster cheese, then another slice of American cheese. Finish with a second slice of bread, butter side up, and cook on medium heat until the bread is toasted and browned on one side and the cheese is starting to melt, 3 to 4 minutes. Flip the sandwich and toast the other side until browned, 3 to 4 minutes more. Transfer the sandwich to a plate, let it sit for 2 minutes so the cheese sets a bit, then cut it in half diagonally. Serve immediately.

BREADS:

Brioche

Caraway rye

Challah

Cinnamon-swirl
bread

Marble rye

Pumpernickel

Raisin bread

Sourdough

Texas Toast

Tortilla

Wheat bread

White bread

Danish rye

Pretzel roll (page 67)

**CHEESES (PICK
ONE OR MORE):**

American

Brie

Cheddar

Chihuahua

Cream cheese

Crumbled blue

Crumbled goat

Emmental

Gouda

Gruyère

Mascarpone

Muenster

Swiss

Provolone

Colby

Monterey Jack

Havarti

**SPREADS &
SPRINKLES:**

Black pepper

Cranberry sauce

Fig jam

Garlic butter

Hoisin sauce

Horseradish Sour
Cream (page 52)

Mango-Tomato
Chutney (page 44)

Mayo

Mustard (grainy,
Dijon, brown, or
honey)

Olive tapenade

Pineapple salsa

Tomato Salsa (such
as Simmered Tomato
Salsa on page 45, or
your favorite prepared
tomato salsa)

Truffle oil

ADD-INS:

Apple slices

Avocado

Bacon

Basil leaves

Caramelized onions

Chopped banana
peppers

Fried egg

Ham

Jalapeños

Pear slices

Pickled vegetables
(page 32)

Roasted Eggplant
Spread (page 49)

Salami

Sauerkraut

Sautéed mushrooms

Spinach leaves

Tomato slices

Grilled Muenster Cheese & Roasted Vegetable Sammie

MAKES 1 SANDWICH

When I was nineteen, living in Cleveland and attending art school, I got my start in the kitchen at the Light of Yoga Good Food Store and Restaurant—though it was by force, not by choice. I was perfectly happy waitressing there for $1.00 an hour, plus tips and the free family meal. But one day one of the line cooks didn't show up for work and my manager asked, "Gale, can you cook?" I said no, I was from the North Shore of Chicago where the only thing we made were reservations. She didn't accept that answer. She threw an apron at me and said, "You can cook now—get in the kitchen!" I was terrified for about four seconds. And then a calm came over me. It was as if I had found my home, as if I were speaking a language I was fluent in but didn't remember learning. I wish I could find that manager now and thank her for the gift she gave me.

My favorite sandwich from my time there, the Rama, was a broiled tomato and Muenster sandwich with oregano and alfalfa sprouts. This sandwich pays homage to the Light of Yoga version.

1 tablespoon extra-virgin olive oil, plus more for the baking sheet

1 medium zucchini, cut lengthwise into ¼-inch-thick strips

½ red bell pepper, sliced into rings

1 medium onion, sliced into rings

1 Japanese eggplant, cut lengthwise into ¼-inch-thick strips

2 cloves garlic, smashed

1 large pinch fresh or dried thyme

1 large pinch dried oregano

Salt and freshly ground black pepper

2 teaspoons unsalted butter

2 slices pumpernickel bread

4 slices Muenster cheese

Two ¼-inch-thick slices heirloom tomato

Heat the oven to 350 degrees. Oil a baking sheet with olive oil.

Arrange the zucchini, bell pepper, onion, eggplant, and garlic on the baking sheet in one layer. Drizzle the vegetables with the olive oil, then sprinkle them evenly with the thyme, oregano, and salt and pepper to taste. Roast the vegetables for 30 minutes, until cooked through. Let the vegetables cool on the pan for 15 minutes, then use them to build the sandwich, or chill them, covered, until ready to use, or for up to 3 days.

Butter each slice of bread on one side. Place one slice, butter side down, in a sauté pan, then layer on 2 slices of the cheese, the roasted vegetables, the tomato slices, and finally the remaining 2 slices cheese. Top with the remaining slice of bread, buttered side up, and cook over medium heat until the bread is toasted and browned on one side and the cheese is melted, 4 to 5 minutes. Flip the sandwich and toast the other side until browned, 4 to 5 minutes more. Remove the sandwich to a plate and cut in half on a slight diagonal. Serve immediately.

Classic Lobster Roll

MAKES 2 SANDWICHES

*It only takes one trip to Kennebunkport, Maine, to fall in love with lobster rolls. That's
what happened to me at the end of one summer. Thirteen of us descended upon the
town for our annual summer family vacation. For five days straight, we ate lobster rolls
anywhere and everywhere we could find them, and never tired of the taste of creamy lobster
salad piled into a toasted bun. I came up with this recipe after that trip, with the help of my
chef friend Dan Smith (cofounder of Hearty Boys, a Chicago catering company). He's from
Maine, so lobster rolls are practically running through his veins. If possible, eat this with
the sound of the sea in your ears. Lobster rolls taste even better that way!*

One 1- to 1½-pound boiled lobster (see
  Note), claw, knuckle, and tail meat
  removed and cooled; 8 ounces fresh
  lobster meat; or 8 ounces frozen lobster
  meat, thawed

¼ cup mayonnaise

1 teaspoon freshly squeezed lemon juice

2 tablespoons minced celery

3 grinds black pepper

1 teaspoon chopped fresh tarragon
  (optional)

2 hot dog rolls (the best quality you
  can find)

2 teaspoons unsalted butter, softened

In a bowl, combine the lobster meat with the mayonnaise, lemon juice,
celery, pepper, and tarragon, if using, and gently stir to combine. Cover
and chill for at least 1 hour or overnight. When ready to eat, split the
bun open, butter it lightly on the inside, and toast it in a toaster oven,
then pile on the lobster salad.

Note: To cook a lobster, fill a large pot three-quarters full with water and salt it
heavily (2 tablespoons salt per 1 quart water). It should taste like seawater (you
can even use clean seawater if you have access to it!). Bring the water to a boil, then
plunge the lobster in headfirst. Place a lid on the pot and boil for 12 to 15 minutes.
The lobster's shell will turn bright red. Remove the lobster from the pot and plunge
it into ice water to chill it quickly and stop the cooking. Remove all the meat from the
shell and use it immediately, or store it in an airtight container in the refrigerator for
up to 3 days.

PACK IT TO GO WITH:
*a tangelo and red and green bell
pepper rings*

EAT IT AT HOME WITH:
*cucumber and tomato
chunks dressed with Mustard
Vinaigrette (page 162)*

MAKE IT A PARTY WITH:
*Potato Leek Soup (page 106)
and Sparkling Strawberry Lime
Lemonade (page 236)*

Egg Salad 101

Basic egg salad is just chopped hard-boiled eggs, celery for crunch, a little salt and pepper for seasoning, and mayonnaise for binding. If you like a little sharpness, you can add 1 teaspoon yellow mustard, or try the same amount of Dijon mustard for more bite. You could also mix things up by adding 1 teaspoon curry powder, or dill weed, or chopped cooked bacon, or chopped roasted red pepper. To lighten the salad, try plain yogurt instead of mayonnaise, and for a crunchy replacement for the celery, try chopped fennel, drained canned water chestnuts, or chopped green bell pepper.

Gale's Egg Salad

MAKES 2 SANDWICHES

My husband and kids (even my picky eater—yes, I have one!) all love egg salad. We use it in sandwiches, of course, but sometimes we serve it in bowls and tuck some crackers next to it, then spoon it onto the crackers. Other times, we make cucumber boats by halving cucumbers and scraping out the seeds, then fill the cavity with egg salad. Any way you serve it, it's bound to go quickly! It keeps well for up to 3 days, so make enough to last you that long. (This recipe can be doubled.)

4 hard-boiled large eggs (page 88), chilled and then peeled under cold water

One 6-inch stalk celery

1 pinch salt

2 grinds black pepper

$\frac{1}{4}$ cup mayonnaise

4 slices hearty white bread, for sandwiches (optional)

Sliced heirloom tomato (optional)

Arugula or watercress (optional)

With a large knife or egg slicer, chop the eggs and place them in a bowl. Cut the celery lengthwise into $\frac{1}{4}$-inch strips, then cut the strips crosswise into $\frac{1}{4}$-inch chunks and place them in the bowl with the eggs. Add the salt, pepper, and mayonnaise, and use a fork to stir everything together. Cover and chill until ready to serve. (The egg salad will keep in an airtight container in the refrigerator for up to 3 days.)

To make sandwiches, lightly toast the bread. Cover one side of one slice of bread with half the egg salad, and cover the egg salad with thin slices of heirloom tomatoes and some peppery greens like arugula or watercress. Top with another slice of toasted bread. Repeat with the remaining ingredients to make a second sandwich. Cut the sandwiches in half down the middle—if you slice this one corner to corner, you might lose some egg salad at the corners! Serve immediately, or wrap and chill until ready to serve.

How to Cook the Perfect Hard-boiled Egg

Over the years I've refined my method for cooking hard-boiled eggs. I started with Julia Child's technique of bringing the eggs to a boil in water, then turning off the heat and letting the eggs sit for 5 minutes, but the yolks can be too soft for egg salad with this method. So I added a little cooking time and a shock of cold at the end to help the shells release easily. Here's what I do:

Have about 8 cups of ice ready. Place 1 or more eggs (I make up to 10 at once) in a saucepan and fill the pan with enough cool water to cover the eggs by 1 inch. Place the pan over high heat and bring the water to a boil. Once the water reaches a rolling boil, turn the heat down slightly so the water is at a gentle boil, and keep at a gentle boil for 6 minutes. After 6 minutes, turn off the heat, pour the boiling water into the sink, and cover the eggs (still in the pan) with ice. Top the ice off with cold water. Let the pan sit until the ice has melted. (This will help the shells separate more easily from the egg whites.) Remove the eggs from the pan and chill the eggs overnight if you have time. I mark my hard-boiled eggs with an X so I don't mix them up with raw eggs.

Peel the hard-boiled eggs under cold running water to make sure any small pieces of shell are removed. You can store peeled eggs in enough water to cover in an airtight container in the refrigerator for up to 2 days. Unpeeled eggs will keep in an airtight container in the refrigerator for up to 5 days.

Bertha's Tuna Salad

MAKES 2 SANDWICHES

When I was a little girl, a warm, wonderful woman named Bertha came to help my mother with the house and kids once a week, on Fridays. She made me lunch every Friday and this is the sandwich I always requested. I still think it's the best possible version of tuna salad, with so much flavor from the red onion and sweet relish. No other tuna salad I've tried tastes as good. Thank you, Bertha May Smith.

1 can chunk white tuna in water, drained well

2 tablespoons finely chopped red onion

1 tablespoon sweet pickle relish

¼ cup mayonnaise

4 slices bread of your choice (I use good white bread), lightly toasted

2 leaves iceberg lettuce

In a medium bowl, combine the tuna, onion, relish, and mayonnaise and mix gently with a fork. Use immediately, or store in an airtight container in the refrigerator until ready to use, or for up to 4 days.

Spread half the tuna salad on one slice of toast, place the lettuce leaves on top of that, and top with another piece of toast. Repeat with the remaining tuna salad and toast to make a second sandwich. Cut the sandwiches in half diagonally, from corner to corner, just as Bertha did, because it's easier to eat a sandwich cut that way! Serve immediately, or wrap and chill until ready to serve.

PACK IT TO GO WITH:
potato chips (of course!)

EAT IT AT HOME WITH:
sweet pickles and baby carrots

MAKE IT A PARTY WITH:
Burrata with Grape Tomato and Celery Salad (page 163) and Matzo Ball Soup (page 109)

Chicken Salad Sliders

MAKES 6 SMALL SANDWICHES; SERVES 2

Sliders are mini cheeseburgers on a small bun that just slide down your throat, but they don't have *to be cheeseburgers. Try putting chicken salad on small buns or rolls, and watch people gobble them up! I like making this with Classic Chicken Salad (page 173), but feel free to switch it out for one of the other chicken salads in the book (or your own version!).*

6 Parker House rolls, mini hamburger buns, or other small soft rolls

2 cups Classic Chicken Salad (page 173), or chicken salad of your choice

6 slices good-quality tomatoes

6 small lettuce leaves

PACK IT TO GO WITH:
a handful of almonds

EAT IT AT HOME WITH:
Crispy Roasted Chickpeas (page 23)

MAKE IT A PARTY WITH:
Parmesan–Black Pepper Popcorn (page 22), Coconut Pecan Crunch Cookies (page 211), and Sauvignon Blanc Spritzers (page 241)

Split the rolls open and toast them, if desired. Place about ⅓ cup chicken salad on the bottom half of each bun, and top it with 1 tomato slice, 1 lettuce leaf, and the top half of the bun. Repeat with the remaining buns, chicken salad, tomato slices, and lettuce leaves. Serve immediately.

Fried Chicken & Waffle Sandwiches

MAKES 6 SANDWICHES

My mom, Myrna, used to make the best fried chicken for us to take on picnics. That's where my love affair began. Fried chicken is something I know about and care about—a lot. I sample fried chicken often, and I probably try six to eight new recipes for it every year, always striving to find the perfect recipe. Here's one that works beautifully for this sandwich, a take on the classic chicken and waffles.

FOR THE CHICKEN
2 boneless chicken breasts, skin on
2 boneless chicken thighs, skin on
Salt and freshly ground white pepper
1 cup buttermilk
1 tablespoon Tabasco sauce
Canola oil, for frying

2 cups all-purpose flour
2 tablespoons Lawry's Seasoned Salt
2 teaspoons freshly ground black pepper

¼ cup mayonnaise
½ teaspoon Tabasco sauce
3 Homemade Waffles (page 93), quartered

Make the chicken: Season the chicken well with salt and white pepper on both sides and let sit for 5 minutes. Place the chicken pieces in a resealable bag with the buttermilk and Tabasco and seal the bag. Let the chicken marinate in the refrigerator for at least 2 hours and up to 24 hours.

Pour ½ inch of canola oil into an iron skillet or large frying pan and heat over medium heat for about 4 minutes, until very hot (275 degrees on a frying thermometer).

In a bowl, mix together the flour, Lawry's Seasoned Salt, and black pepper. Take the chicken pieces out of the buttermilk mixture and dredge them in the flour mixture.

Carefully place the floured chicken pieces into the hot oil and fry each side until golden brown and crispy, about 15 minutes total. Remove the chicken pieces from the hot oil with tongs and set aside to drain on a brown paper bag or paper towels. (The fried chicken will keep in an airtight container in the refrigerator for up to 5 days.)

Mix the mayonnaise with the Tabasco in a small bowl until thoroughly combined.

Cut the breasts in half lengthwise and place one half breast or one thigh on top of a waffle quarter, drizzle it with the mayonnaise mixture, and top it with another waffle, just like a sandwich. Serve immediately.

PACK IT TO GO WITH:
applesauce

EAT IT AT HOME WITH:
Homemade Ginger Ale (page 241)

MAKE IT A PARTY WITH:
Garden Vegetable Coleslaw (page 185) and Chocolate Pudding in a Jar (page 220)

Homemade Waffles

MAKES THREE 7-INCH ROUND WAFFLES

In a medium bowl, stir together the flour, cornmeal, sugar, baking powder, salt, and pepper. In another bowl, whisk together the eggs and the buttermilk. Add the flour mixture to the buttermilk mixture and stir until almost combined (the batter should be lumpy). Stir in the melted butter, being careful not to overmix the batter.

Spray a waffle iron with nonstick cooking spray. Pour ¼ cup of the batter onto the waffle iron and cook according to the manufacturer's instructions.

1 cup all-purpose flour

½ cup yellow cornmeal

2 teaspoons sugar

1 tablespoon baking powder

1 teaspoon salt

¼ teaspoon freshly ground black pepper

2 large eggs

1 cup buttermilk

4 tablespoons unsalted butter, melted

Soups

Gale's Gazpacho

Watermelon Gazpacho

Tomato Soup with Basil & Parmesan Cream

Summer Garden Vegetable Soup

Five-Bean Soup

Four-Bean Vegetable Chili

Butternut Squash & Apple Soup

Corn Chowder

Potato Leek Soup

Chicken & Dumpling Soup

Matzo Ball Soup

Chicken Stock

Gale's Gazpacho

SERVES 4 TO 6

This fresh, easy chilled tomato soup is one of the first things I learned to make. It's what I served for my parents the first time they came to my place for dinner, when I was nineteen and away at art school, and I love that the recipe is still a favorite of mine today, more than thirty-five years later. The mix-ins listed below are merely suggestions—have fun playing around with whatever additions you like. I even topped this soup with popcorn once, when my college budget was tight!

FOR THE GAZPACHO

3 medium tomatoes, chopped
½ seedless (English) cucumber, chopped
1 green bell pepper, seeded and chopped
4 cups chilled tomato juice
¼ cup extra-virgin olive oil
1 tablespoon red wine vinegar
2 tablespoons chopped onion
1 teaspoon dried oregano
½ teaspoon salt
3 dashes Tabasco sauce
3 grinds black pepper

MIX-INS

Cottage cheese
Plain yogurt
Sour cream
Celery slices
Cucumber cubes
Diced yellow tomatoes
Diced red peppers
Croutons
Snipped fresh chives
Fresh cilantro leaves

Combine the tomatoes, cucumber, bell pepper, 1 cup of the tomato juice, the olive oil, vinegar, onion, oregano, salt, Tabasco, and black pepper in a blender and blend on high until completely pureed. Pour the gazpacho into an airtight container, cover, and chill for 30 minutes.

While the soup chills, place your desired mix-ins in small bowls for serving (or containers for transporting, if the soup will be served at a picnic or packed for lunch).

Pour the chilled gazpacho into a pitcher (or a thermos, if transporting) and stir in the remaining 3 cups tomato juice. Fill soup bowls with the gazpacho, leaving room for mix-ins. The gazpacho will keep in an airtight container in the refrigerator for up to 3 days.

PACK IT TO GO WITH:
Chive Crackers (page 27)

EAT IT AT HOME WITH:
Grilled Muenster Cheese and Roasted Vegetable Sammie (page 82)

MAKE IT A PARTY WITH:
Asparagus Risotto with Chives (page 124), Chocolate Pudding in a Jar (page 220), and cinnamon coffee (just throw a cinnamon stick or a shake of ground cinnamon in the coffee maker's filter)

Watermelon Gazpacho

SERVES 4 TO 6

Here's a light and refreshing cold soup that's portable and full of satisfying texture. The bright, fresh flavors of the blushing fruit "broth" really accentuate the crunch and color of the added vegetables and fruit. Feel free to experiment with adding different goodies—maybe some dried fruits or vegetable chips, like the kale chips on page 20.

FOR THE GAZPACHO

3 cups watermelon cubes, seeded

1 cup fresh or canned pineapple chunks (drain if canned)

1 pinch salt

3 grinds black pepper

1 teaspoon roughly chopped fresh tarragon leaves

GARNISHES

½ cup seeded and cubed yellow tomato

½ cup seeded and cubed red tomato

½ cup cubed fennel

½ cup cubed seedless (English) cucumber

1 green apple, cored and cubed

PACK IT TO GO WITH:
bagel chips and cottage cheese

EAT IT AT HOME WITH:
a Ginger Peach Muffin (page 66) spread with ricotta

MAKE IT A PARTY WITH:
Spanish Tortilla (page 153) and Tangerine Ginger Angel Food Cake (page 232)

Place the watermelon and pineapple in a blender and pulse to puree. Stir in the salt, pepper, and tarragon, then transfer the gazpacho to a pitcher or a bowl with a pour spout. Cover the gazpacho and keep it chilled until ready to serve. Chill the prepared fruit and vegetables.

To serve, pour the gazpacho into clear bowls or glasses with handles. Garnish each serving with a few cubes of each vegetable and fruit, or set the cups of soup out on a buffet with the vegetables and fruit in small bowls alongside, and let people garnish their own servings. The gazpacho will keep in an airtight container in the refrigerator for up to 3 days. The chopped fruits and vegetables are best prepared the day you are serving the gazpacho, but they will also keep in airtight containers in the refrigerator for up to 3 days.

Tomato Soup with Basil & Parmesan Cream

SERVES 4 TO 6

In the Midwest, our prime tomato season comes in late August and lasts into September, and during that time there are so many great varieties available at farmers' markets (and even grocery stores). I sometimes ask for the "seconds," or bruised tomatoes, to save a few dollars if I'll just be cutting them up for this soup. In warmer months, this soup tastes great chilled. I always freeze some for later in the year too.

FOR THE TOMATO SOUP

1 tablespoon extra-virgin olive oil

1 medium onion, chopped

3 cloves garlic, sliced

2 pounds ripe heirloom or vine-ripened tomatoes, halved, seeded, and chopped

8 fresh basil leaves, torn into small pieces

Leaves from 1 sprig fresh thyme

2 cups tomato juice

1 cup chicken stock (page 112)

Salt and freshly ground black pepper

FOR THE BASIL AND PARMESAN CREAM

1 cup heavy cream

6 fresh basil leaves, chopped

¼ cup freshly grated Parmesan cheese

Make the tomato soup: In a large pot, heat the olive oil over medium heat. Add the onions and cook, stirring occasionally, until they are translucent, about 5 minutes. Add the garlic and cook, stirring, for 1 minute more. Add the tomatoes, basil, and thyme and cook for about 10 minutes, until the tomatoes soften and start to exude some of their juices. Add the tomato juice and chicken stock and cook for 30 to 40 minutes more to thicken. Puree the soup with an immersion blender (or let cool for 20 minutes then puree it in a blender in batches) and season to taste with salt and pepper. (The soup can be chilled or frozen at this point. It will keep in an airtight container in the refrigerator for up to 5 days or in the freezer for up to 2 months.)

Make the basil and Parmesan cream: Place the heavy cream, basil, and Parmesan in a blender and puree them until well combined. Use the cream immediately or refrigerate it in an airtight container until ready to serve, up to 8 hours.

When ready to serve, warm the soup in a saucepan. Ladle the soup into bowls and stir some of the basil and Parmesan cream into each bowl so it shows in swirls on the surface.

PACK IT TO GO WITH:
sliced salami or pepperoni and crackers

EAT IT AT HOME WITH:
Cheesy Focaccia Sticks (page 40)

MAKE IT A PARTY WITH:
grilled cheese sandwiches (page 81)

Summer Garden Vegetable Soup

SERVES 4

I love creating soups, especially during the summer when my garden is at its peak, producing almost more than I can use. I start the same way every time—I heat some olive oil, then sauté anything that benefits and sweetens from the heat. Then I add some wine and reduce it, then add all the ingredients that just need stewing and cooking down, then some herbs (or "herbage," as I like to call it), and finally some salt and pepper to bring it together and bring out the flavors. This is a delicious recipe, but please feel free to adjust the vegetables based on what's available in your garden or at the market.

2 tablespoons extra-virgin olive oil

1 medium onion, chopped

2 large carrots, halved lengthwise and sliced

2 stalks celery, halved lengthwise and sliced

2 medium zucchini, halved lengthwise and sliced

2 cloves garlic, minced

1/2 cup white wine

4 cups vegetable stock or chicken stock (page 112)

8 large tomatoes (preferably heirloom), coarsely chopped

6 fresh basil leaves, torn into 1/2-inch pieces

1 teaspoon chopped fresh rosemary

1/2 teaspoon fresh thyme leaves

1 bay leaf

Salt and freshly ground black pepper

PACK IT TO GO WITH:
oyster crackers

EAT IT AT HOME WITH:
Chicken Salad (page 173) on challah bread

MAKE IT A PARTY WITH:
Cuban Sandwiches (page 79)

In a large heavy-bottomed pot, heat the olive oil over medium heat. Add the onion and cook, stirring, for 3 to 4 minutes, then add the carrots and celery and continue cooking for about 5 minutes more. Add the zucchini and cook, stirring occasionally, for 5 minutes more. Add the garlic and cook, stirring, for about 1 minute (this gets rid of the garlic's bite), then add the white wine and cook until it has reduced and thickened slightly, about 5 minutes. Add the stock and tomatoes and bring the mixture to a gentle boil, then reduce the heat to low. Add the basil, rosemary, thyme, and bay leaf, and let the soup simmer for about 20 minutes to tenderize the tomatoes and cook them down a bit. Taste the soup and season with salt and pepper. Cook for another 10 minutes or so, then remove and discard the bay leaf. Serve immediately, or allow to cool, then store in airtight pint containers in the refrigerator for up to 5 days or in the freezer for up to 1 month.

Five-Bean Soup

SERVES 6 TO 8

This soup makes my house smell so good when it's cooking on the stove, which in turn makes me feel really nurtured. It's like magic—maybe they're magic beans? This is also a great forum for playing with all the beautiful heirloom bean varieties available. Some of my favorite varieties are cranberry, scarlet runner, Christmas lima, Butterscotch Calypso, and the French classic flageolet. You can also find heirloom bean blends at gourmet food markets and online. Try to mix different sizes, shapes, and colors for the best results.

½ cup each of 4 different dried bean varieties (such as northern, kidney, pinto, and butter, or your favorite heirloom beans) or 2 cups premixed dried bean blend

3 tablespoons extra-virgin olive oil

1 medium onion, chopped

2 carrots, peeled and chopped

2 stalks celery, chopped

8 cups chicken stock (page 112)

1 bay leaf

One 14.5-ounce can diced tomatoes

One 15-ounce can chickpeas, drained and rinsed

Salt and freshly ground black pepper

Place the dried beans in a bowl and add water to cover them by 2 inches. Let the beans soak overnight to soften them up a bit, which helps reduce the cooking time. (If you omit this step, you'll need to cook the soup longer to make the beans tender.) Drain the soaked beans and rinse them. Set aside.

In a large stockpot, heat the olive oil over medium heat. Add the onion, carrots, and celery and cook, stirring, until the onion is translucent. Add the chicken stock, bay leaf, and tomatoes and bring the mixture to a simmer. Reduce the heat to medium-low and continue simmering for 15 minutes.

Add the drained soaked beans and continue cooking, occasionally stirring gently, for 1 to 2 hours, until the beans are tender and soft. Add the chickpeas and cook for 10 minutes more. Taste the soup and season with salt and pepper, then cook for 5 minutes more. Serve hot, or let the soup cool, then store it in airtight containers in the refrigerator for up to 5 days, or in the freezer up to 2 months.

PACK IT TO GO WITH:
grated Parmesan cheese

EAT IT AT HOME WITH:
Chipotle Cheddar Biscuits (page 65)

MAKE IT A PARTY WITH:
Cheesy Focaccia Sticks (page 40) and Simple Green Salad (page 180)

Four-Bean Vegetable Chili

SERVES 6

During the cold autumns and winters we have in Chicago, I'm often in the mood for chili—but I don't always want meat chili. This vegetarian version is one of those recipes that tastes even better the next day, so I love to make a batch (or double it), then divide it into portions to be packed in lunches in the next few days or frozen for future lunches. This chili is delicious topped with grated cheddar, with a corn muffin (page 62) on the side.

2 tablespoons extra-virgin olive oil

1½ bell peppers (use a mix of green, red, yellow, or orange), seeded and diced

1 medium yellow onion, diced

3 large cloves garlic, minced

1 tablespoon chili powder, plus more as needed

½ teaspoon ground cumin

½ teaspoon salt

Two 16-ounce cans diced tomatoes

2 cups fresh, frozen, or canned corn, or one 15-ounce can hominy, drained

One 15-ounce can pigeon peas, drained

One 15-ounce can kidney beans, drained

One 15-ounce can chickpeas, drained

One 15-ounce can black beans, drained

Grated cheddar cheese (optional)

PACK IT TO GO WITH:
Cumin-Spiced Pita Chips (page 30) and grated cheddar cheese

EAT IT AT HOME WITH:
Parmesan–Black Pepper Corn Muffins (page 62)

MAKE IT A PARTY WITH:
Ham and Provolone with Giardiniera (page 78), cut into finger sandwiches, and Tropical Fruit Salad (page 204)

In a large saucepan, heat the olive oil over high heat for 1 minute, then add the bell peppers and onion and cook until the peppers are tender and the onion is translucent, about 3 minutes. Add the garlic, chili powder, cumin, and salt and cook for 1 minute more to "toast" the spices, bringing out more of their flavor. Add the tomatoes and stir. Reduce the heat to medium-low and add the corn, pigeon peas, kidney beans, chickpeas, and black beans. Simmer for about 30 minutes, until the chili has reduced and thickened. Taste for seasoning, adding more chili powder as desired. Serve with grated cheese sprinkled on top, if desired. The chili keeps in an airtight container in the refrigerator for up to 5 days or up to 1 month in the freezer.

Butternut Squash & Apple Soup

SERVES 4 TO 6

The arrival of fall inspires me to cook with all kinds of squash. I encourage you to visit a farm stand and try as many varieties as you can find. I like to cut them in half, remove the seeds, put a little butter in the cavity and seasoning on the cut face, and bake them at 400 degrees until they are fork tender. Or I cut the squash into chunks and toss them with olive oil, salt, and pepper and roast them that way. Or I use them to make this soup! I love using butternut squash in this recipe because it has such a smooth and buttery texture once you puree it, but you can experiment with other varieties of squash too.

2 butternut squash (2 to 3 pounds total)

4 tablespoons unsalted butter, plus more as needed

1 medium onion, chopped

2 stalks celery, chopped

2 carrots, peeled and chopped

2 cloves garlic, chopped

2 apples, peeled, cored, and chopped

2 tablespoons coarsely chopped fresh flat-leaf parsley

½ cup dry white wine

¼ cup cider vinegar

4 cups chicken stock (page 112)

2 teaspoons ground cinnamon

1 teaspoon ground ginger

¼ teaspoon ground nutmeg

⅛ teaspoon ground cloves

Salt and freshly ground black pepper

PACK IT TO GO WITH:
crumbled bacon to sprinkle on top

EAT IT AT HOME WITH:
multigrain baguette slices topped with melted Gouda cheese

MAKE IT A PARTY WITH:
Mustard-Glazed Pork Tenderloin (page 146) and Israeli Couscous with Cranberries and Toasted Pecans (page 119)

Heat the oven to 400 degrees. Cut the squash in half lengthwise and scoop out the seeds. Add ¼ cup water to a roasting pan, then place the squash halves, cut side up, in the pan. Roast until tender, about 30 minutes. Let the squash cool for 5 minutes until they can be handled, then scoop out the softened flesh and set it aside in a bowl.

In a large saucepan, melt the butter over medium heat. Add the onion, celery, and carrots and cook, stirring, until tender, 10 to 15 minutes. Add the garlic and cook for 1 minute more. Add the apples and parsley and cook for about 3 minutes. Add the wine and vinegar and continue to cook until the liquid is almost completely cooked off, 5 to 10 minutes. Add the squash flesh, stock, cinnamon, ginger, nutmeg, cloves, and salt and pepper to taste, and let the mixture simmer for about 30 minutes.

Puree the soup with an immersion blender (or let cool slightly, then puree in batches in a blender) and taste. Add additional salt and pepper, if desired. The soup keeps in an airtight container in the refrigerator for up to 4 days.

Corn Chowder

SERVES 4 TO 6

I make this soup at the end of summer, when corn is at its peak where I live. It also features some of the herbs from what I call my potager garden. (Potager is the French name for a kitchen garden.) If you have any outdoor space near your kitchen, I encourage you to create an herb or vegetable garden, no matter how tiny—even just a few herbs in pots. It's amazing to pick a handful of your own herbs to throw into whatever you're cooking.

½ pound bacon, cut into small pieces

1 small yellow onion, chopped

1 large carrot, peeled, halved lengthwise, and sliced

1 stalk celery, halved lengthwise and sliced

½ bulb fennel, chopped

2 cloves garlic, minced

One 12-ounce can beer (cheap beer is just fine)

½ cup all-purpose flour

6 cups chicken stock (page 112)

3 cups fresh corn kernels (from about 4 ears; reserve the cobs)

2 Yukon gold potatoes, cut into ½-inch cubes

1 tablespoon chopped fresh flat-leaf parsley

1 teaspoon chopped fresh rosemary

½ teaspoon fresh thyme leaves

1 bay leaf

2 cups heavy cream

Salt and freshly ground black pepper

Heat a large heavy-bottomed pot over medium heat. Add the bacon and cook until almost crisp, about 5 minutes. Pour off half of the rendered fat, then add the onion and cook for about 2 minutes, until the onion is slightly shiny.

Add the carrots, celery, and fennel and cook for about 10 minutes, until the vegetables just begin to brown and caramelize. Add the garlic and cook for 1 minute, then add the beer and cook, stirring occasionally, for about 5 minutes, until the liquid has reduced and the mixture has thickened. Add the flour and cook for about 1 minute, then add the stock, corn kernels and corncobs, and potatoes. Bring the mixture to a gentle boil over medium-high heat, then reduce the heat to medium-low and add the herbs. Let the soup simmer for about 20 minutes to tenderize the potatoes and extract flavor from the corncobs. Remove the corncobs, add the cream, and season with salt and pepper to taste. Cook for 10 minutes more. Serve immediately or let cool, then store it in an airtight container in the refrigerator for up to 5 days or in the freezer for up to 2 months.

PACK IT TO GO WITH:
herbed croutons

EAT IT AT HOME WITH:
Wheat Berries with Roasted Brussels Sprouts (page 117)

MAKE IT A PARTY WITH:
Savory Scallion and Bacon Scones (page 68) and Simple Green Salad (page 180)

Potato Leek Soup

SERVES 6

I love the flavor of leeks cooked slowly in butter until they almost seem to melt. And since leeks have a fairly subtle flavor, potatoes are the perfect food to pair them with, as they won't mask the leeks' delicate taste. Leeks are also perfect with other mild ingredients, such as pasta. My husband makes a beautiful pasta dish with leeks, artichokes, lemons, and farfalle, and it's just delightful. (It's also almost the only thing he can cook, but I always say that as long as you have one or two good dishes, you're set. And since he also makes a mean chili once a year, he's set!)

4 tablespoons unsalted butter

2 large leeks, halved lengthwise, sliced, and rinsed of any grit (see Note)

1 stalk celery, halved lengthwise and sliced

2 cloves garlic, minced

1 cup white wine

6 cups chicken stock (page 112) or vegetable stock

3 large Idaho potatoes, peeled and cubed

½ teaspoon fresh thyme leaves

1 bay leaf

2 teaspoons salt, plus more as needed

½ teaspoon freshly ground black pepper, plus more as needed

2 cups heavy cream

2 tablespoons finely snipped fresh chives

1 tablespoon chopped fresh flat-leaf parsley

2 teaspoons chopped fresh tarragon

PACK IT TO GO WITH:
a multigrain roll and trimmed snap peas

EAT IT AT HOME WITH:
sliced Grilled Beef Tenderloin (page 167) on rye bread with Horseradish Sour Cream (page 52)

MAKE IT A PARTY WITH:
Grilled Hanger Steak with Arugula sammies (page 72) and Dried Fruit Salad (page 202)

In a large heavy-bottomed pot, heat the butter over medium heat until it foams. Add the leeks and cook, stirring, until they are translucent and very tender, about 15 minutes. Add the celery and cook for about 5 minutes more. Add the garlic and cook for 1 minute, then add the white wine and cook until the liquid has reduced and the mixture has thickened, about 5 minutes.

Add the stock and potatoes and bring the mixture to a gentle boil, then reduce the heat to low and add the thyme, bay leaf, salt, and pepper. Cook for about 20 minutes to tenderize the potatoes. Remove and discard the bay leaf.

> **❝** I love the flavor of leeks cooked slowly in butter until they almost seem to melt. **❞**

Puree the soup with an immersion blender (or let it cool slightly, then puree it in batches in a blender), then add the cream. Return the pot to the stove over low heat and cook for 5 minutes. Taste the soup and add additional salt and pepper as desired. Stir in the chives, parsley, and tarragon. Serve immediately, or let the soup cool, then store it in airtight pint containers in the refrigerator for up to 4 days or in the freezer for up to 2 months.

Note: To clean leeks, halve them lengthwise and slice them. Then place the slices in a bowl and cover them with water. Drain them into a colander.

Chicken & Dumpling Soup

SERVES 6

My mother, Myrna, often cooked a simple chicken or tomato soup for lunch and then dressed it up by adding spoon-drop dumplings, turning the soup into a main event. These dumplings are easy to prepare, yet they make any soup hearty and heartwarming.

2 tablespoons schmaltz (rendered chicken fat; see Note, opposite) or extra-virgin olive oil

1 medium onion, chopped

2 medium carrots, peeled and chopped

2 stalks celery, chopped

3 Yukon gold potatoes, cubed

8 cups chicken broth (page 112)

1 bay leaf

2 cups torn roasted chicken meat (see page 171)

1 cup fresh or frozen peas

2 tablespoons chopped fresh flat-leaf parsley

Salt and freshly ground black pepper

1 recipe Dumpling Batter (recipe opposite)

PACK IT TO GO WITH:
strawberries

EAT IT AT HOME WITH:
Bertha's Tuna Salad sandwich (page 89)

MAKE IT A PARTY WITH:
Caesar salad and Coconut Pecan Crunch Cookies (page 211)

In a large stockpot, heat the schmaltz or olive oil over medium heat until hot. Add the onion, carrots, and celery and cook, stirring, until the onion is translucent, about 10 minutes. Add the potatoes, stock, and bay leaf and simmer until the potatoes are tender, about 20 minutes. Add the chicken meat and peas and cook a few minutes to thaw the peas. Add the parsley, then taste the soup and season with salt and pepper.

Raise the heat to high and bring the soup to a boil. Scoop about 2 teaspoons (about the size of a large olive) of the dumpling batter onto a spoon and push it into the boiling soup with your finger. Repeat until you've used all the batter. Keep the soup at a boil until all the dumplings rise to the top of the soup, about 2 minutes.

Reduce the heat to medium and cook for 2 to 3 minutes more, until the dumplings are cooked through. (Scoop one out with a slotted spoon and cut it open to make sure it is cooked through to the center; it should be spongy inside.) Remove and discard the bay leaf.

Serve immediately, or let the soup cool, then store it in an airtight container in the refrigerator for up to 3 days.

Dumpling Batter

MAKES ENOUGH FOR 20 SMALL DUMPLINGS

Chicken soup with dumplings is a traditional combination, but you can drop dumplings into just about any kind of soup you like! Be sure the dumplings are cooked through before serving the soup.

In a small bowl, beat the egg with a fork, then add the milk and salt and mix well. Gradually add the flour and mix until you have a smooth, thick batter. Cook as directed.

1 large egg

$\frac{1}{2}$ cup milk

1 teaspoon salt

$1\frac{1}{2}$ cups all-purpose flour

Note: You can make chicken schmaltz yourself—just collect the pan drippings at the bottom of the pan when you make a roasted chicken (page 171). The schmaltz keeps in an airtight container in the refrigerator for up to 2 months. You can also cook down chicken skin and fat in a sauté pan over medium-low heat until it becomes a golden liquid, 20 to 25 minutes, and save that in the refrigerator. Schmaltz can also be found in grocery stores with a good international foods section.

Matzo Ball Soup

SERVES 4

For me, comfort food means matzo ball soup. I used to eat it at Jewish delis and make it at home with my mom, and then I learned how to make it for myself when I was nine or ten years old. My first attempts weren't stellar—let's just say those matzo balls were a little on the firm side. When my brother met his wife-to-be, Joan, she shared her family secret: She adds a touch of extra water to the matzo mixture so it's loose, then lets it rest in the fridge until it firms up enough to form balls that cook up light and fluffy. This soup is still what I like to eat when I'm sick, tired, sick and tired, or just need to feel like my mom is nearby. It gives me comfort in a way nothing else does.

FOR THE MATZO BALLS

1/2 cup matzo meal

2 large eggs, slightly beaten

2 tablespoons schmaltz (see Note, page 109) or vegetable oil

1 teaspoon chopped parsley (optional)

3/4 teaspoon salt

2 grinds black pepper

FOR THE SOUP

6 cups chicken stock (page 112)

1 medium carrot, peeled and sliced crosswise into coins

1 stalk celery, cut crosswise into 1/4-inch slices

Place the matzo meal, eggs, schmaltz, 1/2 teaspoon parsley (if using), salt, pepper, and 1/4 cup water in a medium bowl and use a wooden spoon to mix them together until well combined. Cover and chill the mixture for 30 minutes (or longer), until the matzo absorbs the moisture and the mixture becomes firm.

In a medium saucepan, combine the stock with the carrots and the celery. Bring the soup to a simmer over medium heat, then reduce the heat to medium-low and cook for about 10 minutes to reduce the liquid slightly.

Once the matzo mixture is firm, raise the heat under the soup to medium and bring the soup to a simmer. With wet hands, form 1-inch balls of the matzo mixture, dropping them into the soup as you make them. They will expand as they cook, and float to the surface of the soup once they are cooked through, 5 to 10 minutes. (Scoop one out with a slotted spoon and cut it open to make sure it is cooked all the way through to the center.) Serve immediately, sprinkled with the remaining parsley, or let cool then store in airtight containers in the refrigerator for up to 5 days or in the freezer for up to 2 months.

PACK IT TO GO WITH:
a sesame bagel

EAT IT AT HOME WITH:
half a salami sandwich on rye with coarse-grain mustard

MAKE IT A PARTY WITH:
Turkey Reuben sandwiches (page 74), Dilled Green Beans (page 33), and Lily's Marble Cake (page 231)

Chicken Stock

MAKES ABOUT 8 CUPS

I keep a resealable bag in my freezer where I deposit stock fixings: chicken carcasses from roasted chicken, carrot peelings, onion skins and ends, celery tops, and parsley stems. I often buy chicken stock in boxes to cook with, and keep an open one in my fridge for impromptu pan sauces, but when I have a buildup of chicken bones and vegetables, I like to make my own chicken stock from scratch. The stock makes the house smell wonderful and warm as it cooks.

4 pounds chicken bones (preferably raw; backs and necks are fine), or one 4-pound chicken, cut up, fat removed

2 large carrots, chopped

2 large stalks celery, chopped

2 medium onions, unpeeled, chopped

1 bulb fennel, diced

1 large whole head garlic, unpeeled, halved horizontally

1 bouquet garni (opposite), or 1 bay leaf, 3 sprigs fresh thyme, and 3 sprigs fresh rosemary

1 tablespoon salt

1 teaspoon whole black peppercorns

Rinse the chicken bones under cold water. In a large stockpot, combine the chicken bones with 2 gallons water and set over high heat. Add the carrots, celery, onions, fennel, garlic, bouquet garni, salt, and peppercorns. Cover and let the mixture come to a boil. Reduce the heat to low so that the mixture stays at a bare simmer; do not boil again or the mixture will become cloudy. Simmer, uncovered, for 2 hours, skimming off any foam that rises to the top. When the mixture is golden and lightly flavorful, strain it through a sieve into another stockpot. Discard the solids in the sieve. Skim off any fat that rises to the surface. Use immediately.

If you do not plan on using the stock immediately, set the pot in a sink full of ice water to cool. When the stock is cool, place it in an airtight container in the refrigerator until completely chilled. Remove any fat that rises to or congeals on the surface of the stock. Pour the stock into individual airtight containers (or resealable bags) and freeze as soon as possible. (Alternatively, pour the cooled stock into ice cube trays and freeze. Two ice cubes is the equivalent of about ¼ cup stock.) The stock keeps in the freezer for up to 2 months or in the refrigerator for up to 5 days.

Bouquet Garni

MAKES 1 BOUQUET GARNI

The subtle aromatics in a bouquet garni add depth to soups and stews. This herbal mixture can be adjusted to suit your taste by adding other herbs, such as tarragon, or by adding more chive or bay leaves. Some bouquet garni mixtures include vegetables like carrots and celery, but I prefer to make those vegetables part of the recipe, so I can eat them. Always discard a bouquet garni before serving.

Bundle the thyme, rosemary, bay leaf, parsley, chives, and leek leaves together in a square of cheesecloth or sandwich the herbs inside the leek leaves and tie the bundle together with string or kitchen twine. Drop the bouquet garni into stock or soup to flavor the liquid. Remove and discard the bundle before using the stock or serving the soup.

1 sprig fresh thyme

1 sprig fresh rosemary

1 bay leaf

6 sprigs fresh flat-leaf parsley

4 fresh chives

2 leek leaves, green sections only, rinsed of any grit

Grains

Wheat Berries with Roasted
Brussels Sprouts

Barley with Wild Mushrooms,
Broccoli, & Scallions

Israeli Couscous with Cranberries
& Toasted Pecans

Quinoa with Tomato, Cucumber, & Lemon

Farro with Beet Greens,
Leeks, & Garlic

Wild Rice with Lentils & Spinach

Asparagus Risotto with Chives

Wheat Berries with Roasted Brussels Sprouts

SERVES 4

When I was a child, I wasn't a fan of Brussels sprouts, but now, as an adult, I adore them. In part it's because they look like miniature cabbages, and I like anything mini. But it's also because they are really easy to cook and so satisfying to bite into. Wheat berries have a satisfying texture and nutty flavor that pairs deliciously with the roasted Brussels sprouts.

1 cup wheat berries

2½ teaspoons salt, plus more as needed

1 pound Brussels sprouts, trimmed and halved

4 tablespoons extra-virgin olive oil

¼ teaspoon freshly ground black pepper, plus more as needed

1 yellow onion, chopped

½ cup pine nuts

2 cloves garlic, minced

3 tablespoons freshly squeezed lemon juice

2 tablespoons chopped fresh flat-leaf parsley

Heat the oven to 400 degrees.

Place the wheat berries, 2 teaspoons of the salt, and 4 cups water in a saucepan over high heat and bring the water to a boil. Reduce the heat to medium-low and simmer for 60 to 70 minutes, until the wheat berries are tender. Drain the wheat berries well and set aside to cool in a large bowl.

Place the Brussels sprouts in a roasting pan. Drizzle them with 2 tablespoons of the olive oil, then sprinkle with the remaining ½ teaspoon salt and the black pepper and toss to coat. Roast the Brussels sprouts for 30 minutes, giving them a shake 15 minutes into the roasting time, until they are tender all the way through.

In a sauté pan, heat the remaining 2 tablespoons olive oil over medium heat until hot, about 2 minutes. Add the onion and cook, stirring, until it is transparent, about 4 minutes. Add the pine nuts and cook, stirring, to lightly toast them, about 2 minutes, then add the garlic and cook for 1 minute more. Add the onion mixture to the wheat berries in the bowl and toss to combine. Then add the Brussels sprouts, lemon juice, and parsley and toss again to combine. Taste and season with additional salt and pepper, if desired. Serve warm, at room temperature, or chilled. The wheat berries keep in an airtight container in the refrigerator for up to 3 days.

PACK IT TO GO WITH:
watermelon cubes

EAT IT AT HOME WITH:
Mustard-Glazed Pork Tenderloin (page 146)

MAKE IT A PARTY WITH:
Panko-Crusted Chicken (page 149) and Devil Dogs (page 222)

Barley with Wild Mushrooms, Broccoli, & Scallions

SERVES 4

Barley is a great grain, toothsome and chewy, and I love tossing it with a mix of sautéed vegetables. Try this earthy combination, or use a mix of any leftover vegetables you have on hand!

³/₄ cup pearled barley

1¹/₄ teaspoon salt

2 tablespoons extra-virgin olive oil

1 scallion, sliced

4 cups sliced wild mushrooms (such as shiitake)

¹/₈ teaspoon freshly ground black pepper

2 cloves garlic, minced

2 teaspoons chopped fresh or dried sage

1 cup broccoli florets, blanched in salted water and shocked in ice water

2 tablespoons coarsely chopped fresh flat-leaf parsley

PACK IT TO GO WITH:
Chicken Drumsticks with Chili Sauce (page 150)

EAT IT AT HOME WITH:
Slow-Roasted Salmon (page 160)

MAKE IT A PARTY WITH:
Potato Leek Soup (page 106) and Apple Pie Pops (page 229)

Bring 4 cups water to a boil over high heat. Add the barley and 1 teaspoon of the salt and reduce the heat to low. Simmer for 45 to 50 minutes, until the barley is tender. Drain the barley, then pour it onto a small baking sheet to cool.

Meanwhile, in a large sauté pan, heat the oil over medium heat for about 2 minutes, then add the scallions and the mushrooms and cook, stirring, until the white parts of the scallions are translucent, about 4 minutes. Season with the remaining ¹/₄ teaspoon salt and the pepper. Add the garlic and sage and cook for 1 minute more. Add the cooled barley, broccoli, and parsley, and toss to combine. Serve immediately, or chill before serving. The barley keeps in an airtight container in the refrigerator for up to 3 days.

Israeli Couscous with Cranberries & Toasted Pecans

SERVES 8

I love making this as a side dish to serve with roasted chicken (like the one on page 171) or even Thanksgiving turkey. It's also a perfect lunch dish. Try playing with different combinations of dried fruit and nuts; just be sure to toast the nuts first to bring out more of their flavor and depth. I like to toast the nuts slowly so they don't burn (see page 26). And I keep an eye on them!

2 tablespoons extra-virgin olive oil

2 scallions, sliced

2 cups Israeli couscous

3 cups chicken stock (page 112)

1 teaspoon salt

Grated zest of ½ orange

3 grinds black pepper

¾ cup dried cranberries

1 cup pecans, toasted (see Note, page 26) and chopped

2 tablespoons chopped fresh flat-leaf parsley

In a large sauté pan, heat the olive oil over medium heat for about 2 minutes. Add the scallions and cook, stirring occasionally, until the white parts begin to brown a bit, about 2 minutes. Add the couscous and toast it in the pan until a few pieces turn golden brown, about 3 minutes more. Add the stock, salt, orange zest, and pepper, raise the heat to medium-high, and bring the mixture to a simmer. Cover and reduce the heat to low. Cook until the stock is entirely absorbed and the couscous is tender, about 25 minutes. Remove the pan from the heat and stir in the cranberries, pecans, and parsley. Serve immediately. The couscous keeps in an airtight container in the refrigerator for up to 3 days.

PACK IT TO GO WITH:
shredded Roasted Chicken (page 171)

EAT IT AT HOME WITH:
grilled turkey sausage

MAKE IT A PARTY WITH:
chicken breasts made with the marinade from the Mustard-Glazed Pork Tenderloin (page 146)

Quinoa with Tomato, Cucumber, & Lemon

SERVES 4

This dish is just so delicious and versatile. I've used it as a salad and a passed hors d'oeuvre (presented in an Asian spoon), and served it tucked into a leaf of romaine lettuce. I learned the recipe, with its Turkish-inspired flavors, from Michelle Doll, an expert on gluten-free and allergy-friendly baking and cooking who spent time living in Turkey. We taught cooking and baking classes together at Elawa Farm. Quinoa cooks quickly and is a complete protein, containing all eight essential amino acids—it's a serious superfood!

1 cup pre-rinsed quinoa

1½ cups apple juice

2 tablespoons tomato paste

1 tablespoon paprika

½ teaspoon crushed dried red pepper

Freshly squeezed juice of 1 lemon

¼ cup extra-virgin olive oil

3 scallions, finely chopped

1 large beefsteak tomato, seeded and diced

½ seedless (English) cucumber, diced

¼ cup minced fresh flat-leaf parsley

PACK IT TO GO WITH:
red grapes

EAT IT AT HOME WITH:
Roasted Vegetable Salad (page 194)

MAKE IT A PARTY WITH:
Summer Garden Vegetable Soup (page 100) and ripe raspberries with whipped cream and a drizzle of local honey

Place the quinoa in a small saucepan. Add the apple juice and 1½ cups water and bring to a boil over high heat. Reduce the heat to medium-low and simmer for 12 to 15 minutes, until the quinoa is fully cooked (tender, but still with a bit of chewiness). Drain any excess liquid from the quinoa and set aside to cool.

In a small bowl, combine the tomato paste, paprika, crushed red pepper, lemon juice, and olive oil and whisk until well combined.

In a large bowl, combine the cooled quinoa with the scallions, tomato, cucumber, and parsley. Mix well. Pour the dressing over the quinoa mixture and stir to coat all of the grains. Serve warm, at room temperature, or chilled. The quinoa keeps in an airtight container in the refrigerator for up to 5 days.

Farro with Beet Greens, Leeks, & Garlic

SERVES 4

I was in Italy, in 2001, when I ate farro for the first time. This ancient version of wheat was featured in a cold grain salad and I loved it for its nutty taste and slightly chewy texture. You can toss just about anything (think nuts, dried fruits, and veggies) in with it once the farro is cooked and cooled.

2¼ teaspoons salt

¾ cup farro

¼ cup extra-virgin olive oil

1 leek, halved lengthwise, sliced, and rinsed of any grit (see Note, page 107)

2 cloves garlic, minced

½ pound beet greens, sliced into 1-inch strips

¼ teaspoon salt, or more

⅛ teaspoon freshly ground black pepper

2 tablespoons red wine vinegar

Grated zest of ½ lemon

PACK IT TO GO WITH:
pineapple chunks

EAT IT AT HOME WITH:
Five-Bean Soup (page 101)

MAKE IT A PARTY WITH:
cheesy scrambled eggs and Dried Fruit Salad (page 202)

In a 4-quart saucepan over high heat, bring 4 cups water to a boil with 2 teaspoons salt. Add the farro and reduce the heat to low. Simmer gently until the farro is tender, 45 to 50 minutes. Drain any excess liquid from the farro and spread it on a baking sheet to cool.

In a large sauté pan, heat the olive oil over medium-low heat for 2 minutes. Add the leeks and cook slowly until they are translucent and tender, 15 to 20 minutes. Add the garlic and cook for 1 minute more. Add the beet greens and raise the heat to medium. Cook for 3 to 5 minutes to wilt the beet greens, seasoning them with salt and pepper while they cook. Once the greens are completely wilted and dark green, turn off the heat and let cool for 2 minutes. Add the vinegar and lemon zest and toss, then add the cooled farro and toss again to coat. Serve immediately, or let the mixture cool, then store it in an airtight container in the refrigerator for up to 4 days.

Wild Rice with Lentils & Spinach

SERVES 4

My good friend Janine Gray, who joins me when I walk my dog in the morning, is sometimes my culinary muse, especially when it comes to vegetarian and dairy-free dishes. This one's for you, Janine! It's loaded with legumes, a grain, and vitamin-packed veggies, and its consistency falls in that comforting place somewhere between a soup and a stew.

2 tablespoons extra-virgin olive oil

1 medium onion, chopped

8 ounces sliced mushrooms, such as cremini or baby portobello

2 carrots, peeled and chopped

2 cloves garlic, minced

1½ cups lentils, rinsed and picked through to remove any rocks

½ cup wild rice, rinsed

4 cups vegetable stock

One 15-ounce can diced tomatoes

1 bay leaf

4 cups fresh spinach leaves, or 2 cups thawed frozen spinach

Salt and freshly ground black pepper

In a Dutch oven or large braising pan (something with deeper walls than a sauté pan), heat the olive oil over medium heat for 2 minutes. Add the onion, mushrooms, and carrots and cook, stirring, until the onion is translucent, about 10 minutes. Add the garlic and cook, stirring, for 1 minute more. Add the lentils and wild rice and stir to coat them with the oil, then add the stock, tomatoes, and bay leaf, and reduce the heat to low. Cover and simmer until the lentils and wild rice are tender, about 45 minutes. Stir in the spinach leaves and heat through, then taste the soup and season with salt and pepper. Remove and discard the bay leaf. Ladle the mixture into bowls and serve. This keeps in an airtight container in the refrigerator for up to 4 days.

PACK IT TO GO WITH:
grissini (thin Italian breadsticks)

EAT IT AT HOME WITH:
crusty multigrain bread

MAKE IT A PARTY WITH:
store-bought cheese twists

Asparagus Risotto with Chives

SERVES 4 TO 6

When I make risotto I generally keep it simple to avoid muddling the dish. My mother-in-law, Vita, is my barometer as to whether I've strayed too far from the path to call what I'm making a "risotto." Once she was dining at one of my restaurants and tried our three-grain risotto with mushrooms and artichokes. It had wild rice, barley, Arborio rice, and lentils in it. When asked what she thought of it she said, "I'm sure it's very nice. But it's not risotto." So I kept that in mind when making this more traditional version of the dish, in which you subtly season the pan with shallots, then polish the rice by dressing it with the pan's hot oil, add some spirits and reduce them, then slowly and patiently add stock to coax the rice into toothsome kernels. Fold in just one focal ingredient, herbs, cheese, and a cloud of cream, and you're done! Now that's risotto.

One ¾- to 1-pound bunch asparagus, woody ends trimmed

2 tablespoons extra-virgin olive oil

4 shallots, thinly sliced

2 cloves garlic, minced

2 cups Arborio rice

½ cup dry white vermouth or white wine

6 to 8 cups chicken stock (page 112), warmed

Salt and freshly ground black pepper

1 tablespoon snipped fresh chives, plus more for serving

½ cup freshly grated Parmesan cheese

¼ cup heavy cream, whipped

PACK IT TO GO WITH:
slices of sopressata (Italian salami)

EAT IT AT HOME WITH:
a glass of Pinot Grigio

MAKE IT A PARTY WITH:
Simple Green Salad (page 180) and Parmesan-Crusted Tilapia (page 142; without the topping)

Bring a pot of salted water to a boil (1 teaspoon salt per 6 cups water). Cut the asparagus into 1-inch segments. Add them to the boiling water and cook until tender, about 4 minutes. Drain the asparagus and run some cold water over it to stop the cooking. Set aside.

In a large sauté pan, heat the olive oil over medium heat for 2 minutes. Reduce the heat to medium-low, add the shallots, and cook, stirring, until they are tender and translucent, about 2 minutes. Add the garlic and cook, stirring, for 1 minute more. Add the rice and stir to coat it with the oil. It will turn a little more opaque—this is called dressing or polishing the rice. Add the vermouth and cook until it is reduced to a syrup, 2 to 3 minutes.

> **"** Fold in just one focal ingredient, herbs, cheese, and a cloud of cream, and you're done! **"**

Add about ½ cup of the warm stock to the rice and cook for a few minutes, stirring with a wooden spoon, until the rice has absorbed the stock. Repeat, adding the stock ½ cup at a time, until the rice is still a bit al dente, 20 to 25 minutes. Toward the end of the cooking, taste and season with salt and pepper. Once the rice is cooked, stir in the asparagus, chives, and Parmesan, then fold in the cream. Sprinkle with more snipped chives and serve.

Pasta

Vita's Pasta a Picchi Pacchi
(Pee-key Pah-key)

Mezzi Rigatoni with Gale's Pesto

Baked Ziti with Eggplant, Tomato, & Ricotta

Spaghetti with Goat Cheese,
Wilted Tomatoes, & Chives

Gemelli with Peas & Pancetta

Copperwell Noodles

Vita's Pasta a Picchi Pacchi (Pee-key Pah-key)

SERVES 4

My Sicilian mother-in-law, Vita, who cooks delicious home-style southern Italian food, taught me this recipe. I recently made it as part of a lunch with my brother and sister-in-law, and it was the perfect dish. It's so easy to make—there's almost no prep work! And it's bursting with fresh, honest flavor. That lunch—and this dish in particular—was one of the inspirations for me to write a book filled with delicious lunch recipes.

10 ounces cherry tomatoes (a mix of red and yellow, if available), quartered (or halved, if very small)

1 clove garlic, minced

12 fresh basil leaves, julienned

Salt and freshly ground black pepper

⅓ cup extra-virgin olive oil

½ pound linguine rigatti (linguine with ridges), spaghetti, or fusilli lunghi bucati

½ pound bocconcini (small mozzarella balls), halved

Freshly grated Parmesan cheese

PACK IT TO GO WITH:
fresh fennel sticks

EAT IT AT HOME WITH:
Roasted Vegetable Salad (page 194)

MAKE IT A PARTY WITH:
Pea and Garlic Dip (page 55) on crostini and a bottle of dry rosé

Place the tomatoes in a large bowl. Mix in the garlic, basil, salt and pepper to taste, and the olive oil and let sit for 30 minutes.

Cook the pasta according to the directions on the package. Toss the cooked pasta with the tomato mixture. Add the mozzarella and serve with grated Parmesan sprinkled over the top. This dish keeps in an airtight container in the refrigerator for up to 2 days, but its flavor is best when eaten fresh.

Mezzi Rigatoni with Gale's Pesto

SERVES 2

As my garden winds down each fall, I face the welcome dilemma of deciding what to do with all the basil I have that is still thriving. One of my favorite things to make, of course, is pesto. My pesto features toasted walnuts in addition to the traditional pine nuts. The walnuts give it a nuttier flavor and are a lot more economical. (I also sometimes use butter in place of some of the olive oil, but that's probably just the pastry chef in me.) Here's a simple and delicious way to use pesto.

½ pound mezzi rigatoni (or your favorite tube-shaped pasta, such as cavatappi or penne)

2 tablespoons extra-virgin olive oil

1 small zucchini, sliced crosswise into coins

¼ teaspoon salt

⅛ teaspoon freshly ground black pepper

1 cup grape or cherry tomatoes, halved

½ cup Gale's Pesto (recipe opposite)

PACK IT TO GO WITH:
prosciutto and chilled steamed asparagus

EAT IT AT HOME WITH:
Roasted Eggplant Spread (page 49) on crostini

MAKE IT A PARTY WITH:
Simple Green Salad (page 180) with added artichoke hearts and Chianti Spritzers (page 241)

Cook the pasta according to the directions on the package. In a sauté pan, heat the oil over medium-high heat for 2 minutes, until hot. Add the zucchini and cook, stirring, until tender, 4 to 5 minutes. Season with the salt and pepper. Add the cooked pasta, the grape tomatoes, and the pesto to the pan and toss to coat. Set aside to cool to room temperature and serve, or cover and chill before serving. This keeps in an airtight container in the refrigerator for up to 4 days and is great for lunch when packed in a to-go container. (In a lunch box, add a few slices of rolled up Genoa salami on the side.)

Gale's Pesto

MAKES ABOUT 2 CUPS

Place all the ingredients in a food processor and process until smooth. Refrigerate in an airtight container until ready to use. The pesto will keep in an airtight container in the refrigerator for up to 1 week or in the freezer for up to 2 months. (I pack it in half-pint airtight containers if I'm going to freeze it.)

2 cups packed fresh basil leaves

2 large cloves garlic

½ cup extra-virgin olive oil or 6 tablespoons olive oil and 2 tablespoons unsalted butter

¼ cup walnuts, toasted (see Note, page 26)

¼ cup pine nuts, toasted (see Note, page 26)

½ teaspoon salt

⅛ teaspoon freshly ground black pepper

¾ cup freshly grated Parmesan cheese

Baked Ziti with Eggplant, Tomato, & Ricotta

SERVES 4

My husband, kids, and I go to Naples (Florida, not Italy) to visit my mother-in-law, Vita (source of several delicious recipes), a few times a year. After a long day of travel we are usually greeted with a hot ceramic casserole dish of baked pasta. It might be ziti, or rigatoni, or penne, but it's always dressed in red sauce and topped with melted cheese. The edges get slightly crusty and we fight over who gets that part. There's never any left at the end of the meal. This is my version of her baked pasta, with my personal twist, sautéed eggplant. It's a cozy treat if you're hosting a lunch for friends.

1 large eggplant, peeled

Salt

1 pound ziti

4 tablespoons extra-virgin olive oil

1 medium onion, chopped

2 cloves garlic, minced

One 32-ounce can diced tomatoes

4 fresh basil leaves, torn

Freshly ground black pepper

1 cup ricotta cheese

2 cups shredded mozzarella cheese

1 cup freshly grated Parmesan cheese

PACK IT TO GO WITH: *green bell pepper strips*

EAT IT AT HOME WITH: *steamed broccoli rabe (also known as rapini)*

MAKE IT A PARTY WITH: *Simple Green Salad (page 180) and spinach sautéed with minced garlic*

Cut the eggplant into 1-inch cubes and sprinkle them liberally with salt. Place them in a colander and place the colander on a plate. Let sit for 30 minutes to allow the bitter juices to drain out of the eggplant. Pat it dry.

Heat the oven to 400 degrees.

Cook the pasta until al dente according to the directions on the package. Drain the pasta and rinse it under cold water to stop the cooking. Reserve the pasta in a large bowl.

In a large skillet, heat 2 tablespoons of the olive oil over medium-high heat. Add the eggplant and cook on all sides, until it is just beginning to brown, 10 to 15 minutes. Remove the eggplant from the pan and place it in a 3-quart ovenproof casserole dish.

> **"** The edges get slightly crusty and we fight over who gets that part. **"**

In the large skillet, heat the remaining 2 tablespoons olive oil over medium-high heat. Add the onion and cook, stirring, until it is translucent, about 5 minutes. Add the garlic and cook, stirring, for 1 minute more. Add the tomatoes and cook for about 15 minutes, until they have rendered into a tomato sauce. Add the basil, pepper, and eggplant to the pan and cook for 5 minutes more. Pour the sauce over the pasta and fold to combine. Add the ricotta, 1 cup of the mozzarella, and ½ cup of the Parmesan and fold again to combine. Pour the mixture into the casserole dish and cover the top evenly with the remaining mozzarella and Parmesan. Bake for about 25 minutes, until it is hot and bubbly (and a little crust forms around the edges). Serve hot. The baked ziti keeps, covered, in the refrigerator for up to 4 days.

Spaghetti with Goat Cheese, Wilted Tomatoes, & Chives

SERVES 4

What's better than a vine-ripened cherry tomato? A wilted one, baked in the oven to intensify the flavor, sweeten the starches, and make the texture jammy and tender. Toss wilted tomatoes with good quality pasta, fresh goat cheese, and chives for kick, and you have a perfect simple lunch dish. It's good hot, it's good cold, it's good at home, and it's good to go. If possible, try to make this with goat cheese from a small local farm. One of my favorites is Capriole, in Greenville, Indiana. I love the cheese, and the hospitality of the owner, Judy Schadd.

1 pint red cherry tomatoes

3 tablespoons extra-virgin olive oil

1 clove garlic, minced

¼ teaspoon dried thyme

⅛ teaspoon salt

1 grind fresh black pepper

1 pound spaghetti

4 ounces fresh goat cheese, crumbled

2 tablespoons snipped fresh chives

PACK IT TO GO WITH:
a slice of focaccia

EAT IT AT HOME WITH:
a Citron Pressé (page 243)

MAKE IT A PARTY WITH:
grilled Italian sausage and crostini with Gale's Pesto (page 131)

Heat the oven to 350 degrees.

Place the tomatoes in a roasting pan and drizzle them with 1 tablespoon of the olive oil, then sprinkle them with the garlic, thyme, salt, and pepper, and toss to coat evenly. Roast the tomatoes for 45 minutes to wilt them. They should look wrinkled.

Meanwhile, cook the pasta until al dente according to the directions on the package. Drain the pasta, reserving about ¼ cup of the cooking water. Place the pasta back in the pot with the reserved cooking water, the goat cheese, the remaining 2 tablespoons olive oil, and the chives and toss. Add the wilted tomatoes and toss gently one more time. Taste for seasoning and add salt and pepper if needed. Serve immediately. The spaghetti keeps in an airtight container in the refrigerator for up to 2 days.

Gemelli with Peas & Pancetta

SERVES 4

When my husband and I take our kids to Italy we hear the word gemelli *often. Wherever we go people see us and exclaim, "Gemelli! Gemelli!" Turns out,* gemelli *is the Italian word for twins, and we have twin little girls. There is double-helix shaped pasta that is also called gemelli, so this is a dish for our twin girls, Ruby and Ella, our sweet "gemelli."*

1 cup diced pancetta (about 6 ounces)

1 small onion, diced

1½ cups chicken stock (page 112)

2 cups frozen peas

1 pound gemelli

4 tablespoons (½ stick) unsalted butter

¾ cup freshly grated Parmesan cheese

1 tablespoon chopped fresh flat-leaf parsley

Salt and freshly ground black pepper

In a large sauté pan, cook the pancetta over medium heat until it is almost crispy, about 5 minutes. Add the onions and continue cooking until the pancetta is crispy and the onion is sweet and translucent, 3 to 5 minutes more. Add the stock and the peas and simmer over medium heat for 5 to 10 minutes to reduce the stock.

Meanwhile, cook the pasta until nearly al dente according to the directions on the package. Drain the pasta, reserving ¼ cup of the cooking water, and add the pasta to the sauté pan. Cook it for about 2 minutes in the sauce, stirring gently to coat the pasta. Add the butter, cheese, and parsley and cook, stirring, for 1 minute more. Taste and add salt and pepper if needed. If the sauce is too thick, add a little of the reserved cooking water. The gemelli keeps in an airtight container in the refrigerator for up to 4 days.

PACK IT TO GO WITH:
slices of fontina cheese

EAT IT AT HOME WITH:
Kale Salad with Pine Nuts, Raisins, and Parmesan (page 184)

MAKE IT A PARTY WITH:
zucchini rounds topped with oven-roasted tomatoes and goat cheese (see page 134 of Gale Gand's Brunch! *for recipe)*

Copperwell Noodles

SERVES 1

I love this dish, which features a quick, one-pan Asian noodle sauce. If you're making lunch for just yourself, follow the recipe as-is; you can also double or quadruple it as needed. (One year, I multiplied the sauce recipe by twenty and put it in attractive bottles with resealable lids to have on hand for holiday gifts.) I like making this for dinner and then toting leftovers with me for lunch the next day. I toss linguini, shredded chicken, and shelled edamame with the sauce; feel free to use any leftover meat (julienned pork is good), any sautéed veggie, and then whatever type of noodle you like, whether it's buckwheat soba noodles or Chinese rice stick noodles.

¼ pound linguine

About ⅓ cup Copperwell Noodle Sauce (recipe opposite)

½ cup shredded roasted or poached chicken (see page 171 or 172)

½ cup shelled edamame

PACK IT TO GO WITH:
sliced cucumbers

EAT IT AT HOME WITH:
Chicken Drumsticks with Chili Sauce (page 150)

MAKE IT A PARTY WITH:
Tropical Fruit Salad (page 204) and Homemade Ginger Ale (page 241)

Cook the linguine according to the package directions, then drain it and let it cool to room temperature. Toss the cooked and cooled linguine with the sauce, chicken, and edamame and serve immediately, or pack it in a to-go container. Serve at room temperature.

Copperwell Noodle Sauce

MAKES ABOUT 1½ CUPS

Heat about half of the canola oil in a medium sauté pan over medium heat. Add the cayenne pepper and cook until singed (it goes from red to brown when it's singed). Pour the oil-cayenne mixture into a medium bowl. Heat the remaining canola oil in the same pan over medium heat. Add the sesame seeds and cook, stirring, until they turn golden brown, about 1 minute. Turn off the heat and add the sugar, sesame oil, and scallions and stir to combine and dissolve the sugar. Add this mixture to the oil-cayenne mixture in the bowl, then whisk in the soy sauce and Szechuan pepper. The sauce keeps in an airtight container in the refrigerator for up to 3 weeks.

¾ cup canola oil

½ to ¾ teaspoon ground cayenne pepper

3 tablespoons sesame seeds

4 teaspoons light brown sugar

1 teaspoon sesame oil

¾ cup sliced scallions

½ cup soy sauce

1 teaspoon Szechuan peppercorns, crushed (optional; if using, measure first, then crush with the back of a sauté pan; available from Asian grocery stores)

Entrees

Chicken with Corn & Avocado Salsa

Parmesan-Crusted Tilapia with Cucumber,
Tomato, & Fennel Relish

Grilled Orange-Garlic Shrimp Skewers

Mustard-Glazed Pork Tenderloin

Thai Summer Rolls

Simple Chicken Burritos

Panko-Crusted Chicken

Chicken Drumsticks with Chili Sauce

Grilled Tuna with Cucumber Wasabi Salsa

Spanish Tortilla

Rustic Ratatouille Tart

Sausage & Escarole with White Beans

Chicken with Corn & Avocado Salsa

SERVES 2

I love preparing chicken this way: giving it a light coating of flour, sautéing it, then simmering it in a bit of wine and stock before serving. You can spoon almost any type of sauce over it—here, it's dressed with a chunky, fresh summer salsa. Blistering corn gives it some charred flavor and also makes the corn taste a little sweeter.

FOR THE SALSA

1 tablespoon extra-virgin olive oil

1 cup fresh corn kernels (from about 2 ears), or 1 cup frozen corn

¼ teaspoon salt

⅛ teaspoon freshly ground black pepper

¼ teaspoon ground cumin

1 avocado, pitted, peeled, and cubed

½ cup chopped jarred roasted red pepper

2 tablespoons roughly chopped fresh cilantro leaves

Grated zest of 1 lime

Freshly squeezed juice of 1 lime

FOR THE CHICKEN

Two 6- to 8-ounce chicken breasts

½ cup all-purpose flour

½ teaspoon salt

¼ teaspoon freshly ground black pepper

3 tablespoons extra-virgin olive oil

½ medium red onion, diced

2 cloves garlic, minced

½ cup white wine

1 cup chicken stock (page 112)

Freshly squeezed juice of 1 lime

2 tablespoons unsalted butter

PACK IT TO GO WITH:
a handful of red, orange, and yellow sweet mini peppers (the kind you can eat whole)

EAT IT AT HOME WITH:
yellow rice

MAKE IT A PARTY WITH:
Pineapple Limeade (page 240) and Strawberry Salad (page 205)

Make the salsa: Heat the olive oil in a sauté pan and add the corn, seasoning it with the salt and pepper. Cook, stirring, until the kernels start to brown, 5 to 8 minutes. Add the cumin and cook for 1 minute more to toast the cumin and bring out its flavor. Set aside to cool.

In a bowl, combine the avocado, roasted red pepper, cilantro, lime zest, and lime juice. Add the blistered corn and set aside.

Make the chicken: Slice the chicken breasts at an angle into 5 or 6 cutlets (thin pieces). In a resealable bag, combine the flour, salt, and pepper. Seal the bag and give it a shake to mix the ingredients. Place the chicken pieces in the bag and shake to coat them.

> **❝** You can spoon almost any type of sauce over it—here, it's dressed with a chunky, fresh summer salsa. **❞**

In a large skillet, heat 2 tablespoons of the olive oil over medium heat until very hot, about 2 minutes. Carefully add the floured chicken pieces to the pan and cook until light golden brown on both sides, about 4 minutes per side. Transfer the chicken to a platter.

In the same skillet, heat the remaining 1 tablespoon olive oil over medium heat. Add the onion and cook, stirring, until it is almost translucent, 3 to 5 minutes. Add the garlic and cook, stirring, for 30 seconds. Add the wine and cook until it has reduced by half, about 5 minutes, then add the stock and return the chicken to the pan. Simmer over medium-low heat for about 5 minutes, until the chicken is cooked through and the stock has reduced.

Just before serving, add the lime juice and swirl in the butter. Serve the chicken topped with the salsa. Store the salsa and chicken in separate airtight containers in the refrigerator for up to 4 days.

Parmesan-Crusted Tilapia with Cucumber, Tomato, & Fennel Relish

SERVES 4

A trip to Costa Rica made me mad for tilapia. Here, I bread it lightly with a mixture of panko (my favorite type of bread crumb) and grated Parmesan, which melts and browns and toasts like the best part of a grilled cheese sandwich.

FOR THE FISH
1 large egg

1 cup panko (Japanese bread crumbs)

1/2 cup freshly grated Parmesan cheese

2 teaspoons chopped fresh flat-leaf parsley

1/4 teaspoon freshly ground black pepper

4 tilapia fillets

1/4 cup canola oil

FOR THE RELISH
1/4 seedless (English) cucumber, cut into 1/4-inch cubes

1 heirloom or vine-ripened tomato, seeded and chopped into 1/4-inch pieces

1/2 medium bulb fennel, cut into 1/4-inch pieces

1 scallion, sliced

1 orange, peeled and sectioned

2 tablespoons white wine vinegar

1/4 cup extra-virgin olive oil

1/2 teaspoon salt

1 pinch freshly ground black pepper

1 pinch sugar

6 fresh basil leaves, roughly chopped

PACK IT TO GO WITH:
watermelon wedges and a lime wedge (for squeezing on the watermelon)

EAT IT AT HOME WITH:
couscous

MAKE IT A PARTY WITH:
Delicata Squash with Garlic (page 192) and Coconut Blueberry Tapioca (page 215)

Make the fish: Crack the egg into a wide, shallow bowl, then beat it with a fork with 1 teaspoon water. In another wide, shallow bowl, combine the panko, Parmesan, parsley, and pepper.

Dip the fillets, one at a time, into the egg, coating both sides. Then place them one at a time into the crumb mixture to coat, gently turning them to coat both sides and pressing down a bit to help the crumbs stick to the fish. Place the fillets on a platter.

In a large sauté pan, heat the canola oil over medium-high heat for about 2 minutes. Add the coated fillets and cook until golden brown on one side, about 5 minutes, then carefully flip them and cook until the other side is golden brown, about 5 minutes more.

Make the relish: In a medium bowl, combine the cucumber, tomato, fennel, scallion, orange sections, vinegar, olive oil, salt, pepper, sugar, and basil and toss to mix.

To serve, place the fillets on plates and spoon the relish over them. Store the relish and the fish in separate airtight containers in the refrigerator for up to 3 days.

Grilled Orange-Garlic Shrimp Skewers

SERVES 4

I love my grill. It just seems to make everything taste better. It caramelizes things and lends a touch of charred flavor, and marinating before grilling brings foods to even greater flavor heights. And being as short as I am, I like anything that adds height!

16 U-10 size shrimp (10 to a pound)

¼ cup extra-virgin olive oil

2 or 3 cloves garlic, minced

2 tablespoons chopped fresh flat-leaf parsley

1 orange, zested, then sliced and quartered into wedges

¼ teaspoon salt

⅛ teaspoon freshly ground black pepper

1 green bell pepper, cut into 1-inch chunks

Soak 4 long bamboo skewers in water for 2 hours. (Or use 4 metal skewers thin enough for the shrimp.)

Peel the shrimp and run a knife down their edges to open up the vein, then run cold water over the vein to remove any dirt.

Place the olive oil, garlic, parsley, orange zest, salt, and pepper in a resealable bag and seal it. Massage the bag with your hands to combine the ingredients. Add the shrimp to the bag, seal it, and toss to coat the shrimp with the marinade. Chill for at least 3 hours and up to 24 hours.

When ready to cook, skewer one end of 1 shrimp, then 1 orange wedge, then the other end of the shrimp (so the orange wedge is between the tail and head of the shrimp on the skewer), then 1 piece of green bell pepper, then another shrimp and orange wedge, and repeat until you have 4 shrimp on the skewer. Repeat with the remaining skewers, shrimp, orange wedges, and bell pepper. Lay the finished skewers on a plate and drizzle them with any marinade left in the bag.

Heat your grill to medium, letting it heat for about 5 minutes. Grill the shrimp until both sides are pink and opaque, about 3 minutes per side. Serve hot, or chill, covered, before serving. The shrimp keeps, wrapped well in plastic wrap, in the refrigerator for up to 2 days.

PACK IT TO GO WITH:
a Mandarin orange and a lemon wedge to squeeze over the skewer

EAT IT AT HOME WITH:
mixed greens tossed with Mustard Vinaigrette (page 162)

MAKE IT A PARTY WITH:
stone-ground grits and Cava

Mustard-Glazed Pork Tenderloin

SERVES 4

Marinating pork in a resealable bag makes it extra flavorful, and it has become my new go-to method whether I'm grilling the meat or roasting it in the oven. There are Asian overtones to this marinade—soy, garlic, and ginger—which lend a touch of exotic flavor. I love this pork with the Vinaigrette Potato Salad on page 188—I think pork and potatoes is one of the best culinary combinations around!

2 tablespoons coarse-grain mustard

1 tablespoon soy sauce

1 tablespoon extra-virgin olive oil

Grated zest of ½ orange

1 clove garlic, chopped

½ teaspoon dried thyme

¼ teaspoon ground ginger

⅛ teaspoon freshly ground black pepper

One 1-pound pork tenderloin

PACK IT TO GO WITH:
Honey Crisp apple wedges and multigrain bread, for making a sandwich

EAT IT AT HOME WITH:
boiled red potatoes and coarse-grain mustard

MAKE IT A PARTY WITH:
Maple Sweet Potato Puree with Hazelnuts (page 193)

Combine the mustard, soy sauce, olive oil, orange zest, garlic, thyme, ginger, and pepper in a large resealable bag and seal it. Massage the bag to combine the marinade ingredients well. Open the bag and place the tenderloin inside, then squeeze all the air out of the bag and seal it. Massage the bag again, working the marinade into the pork. Refrigerate for at least 3 hours and up to 2 days, until ready to roast.

Heat the oven to 400 degrees. Remove the pork from the marinade and place it in a small roasting pan (discard the bag of marinade). Roast for 20 to 25 minutes, until the pork reads 140 degrees (at its thickest part) on a meat thermometer. Remove the pork from the oven and let it rest for 10 minutes before slicing it into ¼-inch-thick slices. The pork keeps in an airtight container in the refrigerator for up to 4 days.

Thai Summer Rolls

MAKES 4 ROLLS;
SERVES 2 AS A MAIN COURSE OR 4 AS A SIDE

Although I've cooked in Thailand, I learned how to make these in Chicago—at Lollapalooza. I was working with my farmer friend Pete Klein of Seedlings Farm, making smoothies for his booth. A Thai food booth was next to us, and the family running it made hundreds of these rolls all day long, using a thick slice of a tree covered with a damp towel for their work surface. Since then, I have made them in my kids' cooking classes and in a high school cafeteria, getting kids who had never eaten salad to try them and love them. These rolls are full of flavor and great to pack for a light lunch.

1 cup shredded roasted chicken (page 171)

½ cucumber, cut into 3-inch by ¼-inch sticks

½ carrot, peeled and grated

1 cup torn Bibb lettuce leaves

½ cup bean sprouts

¼ cup soy sauce

2 tablespoons sesame oil

Freshly squeezed juice of 2 limes

¼ cup honey

4 rice paper sheets

¼ cup fresh Thai basil leaves

¼ cup fresh mint leaves

Traditional Thai red chili sauce for dipping (available in most grocery stores)

In a bowl, toss together the chicken, cucumber, carrot, lettuce, and sprouts. In a small bowl, whisk together the soy sauce, sesame oil, lime juice, and honey. Pour the soy sauce mixture over the chicken mixture and toss to coat.

Soak a clean dishtowel with water and ring it out very well. Turn an 8- or 10-inch cake pan upside down and cover it with the towel. Fill a pie plate with warm water.

Dip one of the rice paper sheets into the warm water, moving it around for about 30 seconds, until it becomes translucent. (Do not leave it soaking in the water or it will become too soggy.) Quickly place the rice paper on the towel-covered cake pan and use it immediately. Place one-quarter of the chicken mixture along the front edge of the rice paper, top with a few basil and mint leaves, and roll the rice paper into a tight summer roll shape, tucking the ends in as you roll. Repeat with the remaining rice paper sheets and chicken mixture. Serve at room temperature, with the chili sauce on the side for dipping. The summer rolls keep in an airtight container in the refrigerator for up to 2 days.

PACK IT TO GO WITH:
clementines

EAT IT AT HOME WITH:
Copperwell Noodles (page 136)

MAKE IT A PARTY WITH:
Grilled Orange-Garlic Shrimp Skewers (page 145) and Iced Tea (page 245)

Simple Chicken Burritos

SERVES 2

Sometimes I crave a chicken burrito. And when I do, I want it to include exactly the fillings in my fantasy, so instead of going to a local burrito joint, I roll my own. Feel free to add whatever your favorite fillings are, whether you prefer black beans, some avocado, or a spicier salsa.

Two 10-inch flour tortillas

1 cup shredded or chopped roasted chicken (page 171)

½ cup medium tomato salsa

Salt and freshly ground black pepper

½ cup fresh corn kernals (from 1 to 2 ears) or ½ cup frozen corn

1 cup shredded romaine or iceberg lettuce

4 cherry tomatoes, quartered

½ cup grated cheddar cheese

PACK IT TO GO WITH:
jicama sticks and Herbed Yogurt Dip (page 56)

EAT IT AT HOME WITH:
Gale's Guacamole (page 50) and tortilla chips

MAKE IT A PARTY WITH:
long-grain white rice with cilantro and tortilla chips with Salsa Verde (page 48)

Lay the tortillas flat on a work surface.

In a small bowl, toss the chicken with the salsa. Add salt and pepper to taste. Divide the chicken mixture between the tortillas, placing it in the center of the tortilla. Divide the corn, lettuce, tomatoes, and cheese evenly between the tortillas. Roll up the tortillas by folding in the sides and then rolling from bottom to top. Wrap the burritos in waxed paper or parchment paper to help them keep their shape, and place them on a microwave-safe plate. Microwave for 1 minute. Serve immediately, or wrap the burritos in foil to pack in a lunch box to be eaten later in the day.

Panko-Crusted Chicken

SERVES 4

Fried chicken is one of my favorite foods, and this is a kid-friendly version I've been making lately. It's so simple, but what sets it apart from typical fried chicken is panko, Japanese bread crumbs that are coarser and fluffier than typical bread crumbs. Using panko results in a lighter, crunchier coating. (Panko is available at most supermarkets.) These crispy chicken strips are great for a lunch gathering, and the leftovers are super for packing in a lunch box the next day. My kids love dipping them in applesauce.

3 boneless, skinless chicken breasts

3 cups panko (Japanese bread crumbs)

1 teaspoon salt

¼ teaspoon freshly ground black pepper

4 large eggs

Canola oil, for frying

Trim any fat off the chicken breasts, then cut them lengthwise into strips about ¾ inch wide.

In a large, shallow bowl, combine the panko with the salt and pepper. In a separate large, shallow bowl, combine the eggs with 1 tablespoon water and beat them together with a fork.

Dip the chicken strips in the seasoned panko, making sure to coat all sides, then dip them into the egg, and finally back into the panko for another coating. Pile the prepared chicken strips on a plate.

Meanwhile, heat ⅛ inch of canola oil in a large frying pan over medium heat until very hot. (Test the heat of the oil by placing a chicken strip in the pan; when the oil is hot enough, it will sizzle.) Add the chicken pieces and cook until golden brown on all sides, using tongs to turn the chicken, about 12 minutes total. Transfer the cooked chicken to a paper towel–lined plate. Serve warm. The chicken strips keep in an airtight container in the refrigerator for up to 4 days.

PACK IT TO GO WITH:
Apple Butter (page 57), for dipping

EAT IT AT HOME WITH:
honey mustard, for dipping, and Simple Green Salad (page 180)

MAKE IT A PARTY WITH:
mashed potatoes and corn on the cob

Chicken Drumsticks with Chili Sauce

SERVES 4

After three years at the Cleveland Art Institute, I transferred to the Rochester Institute of Technology's School for American Crafts, which is where I earned my BFA. While I lived in upstate New York, I ate my share of buffalo wings. But it always seemed like a gyp! Eating them required so much work for so little meat. So here's a version that replaces the chicken wings with chicken drumsticks—something a girl can really bite into. They aren't deep-fried because I think it's all about the sauce; I love the hot, spicy flavor and how easy it is to make. And these drumsticks are so portable—perfect for lunch!

8 chicken drumsticks
Salt and freshly ground black pepper
4 tablespoons unsalted butter, melted

¼ cup Tabasco sauce or Frank's Red Hot Sauce
1 tablespoon tomato paste
1 tablespoon cider vinegar

PACK IT TO GO WITH:
celery sticks and Blue Cheese Vinaigrette (page 168), for dipping

EAT IT AT HOME WITH:
a baked potato

MAKE IT A PARTY WITH:
Vinaigrette Potato Salad (page 188), Garden Vegetable Coleslaw (page 185), and Big Chewy Chocolate Chip Cookies (page 210)

Heat the oven to 425 degrees.

Place the chicken drumsticks on a baking sheet and season them on all sides with salt and pepper. Bake for 30 to 35 minutes, until the juices running out are clear.

Meanwhile, in a large bowl, whisk together the butter, Tabasco, tomato paste, and vinegar. As soon as the drumsticks come out of the oven, place them in the bowl with the sauce and, using a pair of tongs, toss them to coat. Return them to the oven to bake for 5 minutes, then toss them again with the remaining sauce. Serve hot or cold. The drumsticks keep in an airtight container in the refrigerator for up to 1 week.

Grilled Tuna with Cucumber Wasabi Salsa

SERVES 4

I love crunchy, summery, fresh salsa over grilled fish. You can easily make this a gluten-free dish by replacing the regular soy sauce with gluten-free soy sauce or gluten-free tamari. When I grate ginger for a marinade, I like to use a Microplane to get it nice and fine. You can use a Microplane for your garlic too, if you don't feel like mincing it.

FOR THE TUNA

2 tablespoons extra-virgin olive oil

2 tablespoons soy sauce or tamari

2 cloves garlic, minced

1-inch piece fresh ginger, peeled and grated

Grated zest of 1 clementine (reserve the fruit for the salsa)

Four 4- to 6-ounce tuna steaks

FOR THE SALSA

¼ seedless (English) cucumber, peeled and cut into ¼-inch cubes

½ jicama, peeled and cut into ¼-inch cubes

½ teaspoon powdered wasabi or wasabi paste from a tube

2 tablespoons rice wine vinegar

¼ cup extra-virgin olive oil

½ teaspoon salt

1 pinch sugar

PACK IT TO GO WITH:
rice crackers

EAT IT AT HOME WITH:
steamed sticky rice

MAKE IT A PARTY WITH:
Roasted Vegetable Salad (page 194) and fortune cookies

Make the tuna: Place the olive oil, soy sauce, garlic, ginger, and orange zest in a resealable bag and seal it. Massage the bag to combine the ingredients. Place the tuna in the bag, reseal it, and tumble to coat the tuna with the marinade. Let it sit for 30 minutes at room temperature to marinate, or refrigerate for up to 8 hours.

Heat your grill to medium. When the grill is hot, remove the tuna from the bag and place it on the grill for 3 to 4 minutes per side, 6 to 8 minutes total, depending on how rare or well done you like your tuna.

Make the salsa: Place the cucumber and jicama in a small bowl. Remove any remaining peel from the reserved clementine. Separate the segments and chop them into small pieces. Add them to the bowl with the cucumber and jicama.

In a separate small bowl, whisk together the wasabi powder, vinegar, olive oil, salt, and sugar. Toss the wasabi mixture with the cucumber mixture.

To serve, place one tuna steak on each of 4 plates and top with the salsa. Store the tuna and the salsa in separate airtight containers in the refrigerator for up to 3 days.

Spanish Tortilla

SERVES 4

I first had this dish in Spain when I went to Barcelona just before the Olympics in 1992. I was working in England at the time, and one of the great things about England is that Spain (not to mention France) is so close. This became one of my favorite dishes. And then my chef friend Elizabeth Brown shared her wonderful recipe for it with me. We were on the Marshall Field's Culinary Counsel together and traveled the country doing in-store cooking demonstrations. I was always happy when she taught this dish. I love how easy it is to prepare and how delicious it is to eat. It's like a thick Italian frittata, but with potatoes, onions, and peppers in the egg mixture instead of pasta.

½ cup plus 4 tablespoons extra-virgin olive oil

½ onion, chopped

½ green bell pepper, seeded and chopped

½ red bell pepper, seeded and chopped

1½ pounds frozen cubed potatoes

4 large eggs

1½ teaspoons salt

¼ teaspoon freshly ground black pepper

In a nonstick skillet, heat ½ cup of the olive oil over medium-high heat. Add the onions and peppers and cook until the onions are almost translucent, about 5 minutes. Add the potatoes and cook, stirring occasionally, until the potatoes are completely thawed and beginning to brown a bit, about 15 minutes. Turn off the heat and let cool slightly.

In a bowl, whisk together the eggs, salt, and pepper, then add the slightly cooled potato mixture. Add 2 tablespoons of the olive oil to the same skillet and heat over medium heat until hot, about 2 minutes. Add the egg mixture and spread it out evenly in the pan. Reduce the heat to low and let the tortilla cook for about 15 minutes, until it is set. Once the tortilla is set, place a large plate over the skillet and carefully invert the skillet and the plate together, in one swift motion, so the tortilla flips onto the plate. Add the remaining 2 tablespoons olive oil to the skillet and heat it over medium heat until hot, about 2 minutes. Slide the tortilla back into the skillet, uncooked side down. Reduce the heat to low and cook for 15 minutes more, until golden brown on the bottom. Cut the tortilla into wedges and serve immediately. The tortilla keeps, covered, in the refrigerator for up to 2 days. Bring to room temperature before eating.

PACK IT TO GO WITH:
Simmered Tomato Salsa (page 45)

EAT IT AT HOME WITH:
a dollop of sour cream and a snip of fresh chives

MAKE IT A PARTY WITH:
plates of sliced Serrano ham and Dates with Goat Cheese (page 38)

Rustic Ratatouille Tart

SERVES 2

This tart is warm, crisp, tender, savory, and caramelized, all at the same time. Using store-bought pie dough makes this recipe really easy, but feel free to make your own crust (see page 230). I think this tart looks gorgeous, so at a lunch party I bring the whole tart to the table on a cutting board and cut it into wedges there. My French friend Muriel taught me how to make ratatouille while we were in college together, and we used to eat it with a fried egg on top. Try topping this one with a fried egg if you want a little extra decadence!

10 ounces cherry tomatoes, halved

1 yellow bell pepper, seeded and chopped

1 small eggplant (about 4 ounces) or a 5-inch section from a Japanese eggplant, cubed

1 zucchini, cubed

1 medium onion, chopped

2 tablespoons extra-virgin olive oil

½ teaspoon salt

⅛ teaspoon freshly ground black pepper

½ recipe Myrna's Pie Crust (page 230), or store-bought pie dough for 1 crust

¼ cup freshly grated Parmesan cheese

Scant 1 cup crumbled goat cheese

3 fresh basil leaves, julienned

2 tablespoons milk

Heat the oven to 400 degrees.

Place the tomatoes, pepper, eggplant, zucchini, and onion on a rimmed baking sheet, drizzle them with the olive oil, and sprinkle with the salt and pepper. Gently toss the vegetables to coat them with the olive oil, being careful not to break them up too much. Roast the vegetables for 30 to 35 minutes, until they are caramelized a bit and have shrunk somewhat but are still moist. Set aside to cool. Leave the oven on.

Line a baking sheet with parchment paper. On a floured work surface, roll out the pie dough into a 13-inch round. Place the round of dough on the lined baking sheet. Leaving a 2-inch rim around the edge, sprinkle 1 tablespoon of the Parmesan over the dough, followed by ½ cup of the goat cheese, then half of the basil, and finally half of the slightly cooled vegetables. Top the vegetables with 1 tablespoon of Parmesan, then the remaining ½ cup goat cheese, the remaining basil, and finally the remaining vegetables. Sprinkle another 1 tablespoon of Parmesan over the filling. Fold the 2-inch edge of the dough over the filling, pleating it as you go around; some of the filling will show in the center. Brush the folded edges with the milk and sprinkle with the remaining Parmesan. Bake for 35 to 45 minutes, until the crust is golden brown. Cut the tart into wedges and serve immediately.

PACK IT TO GO WITH:
Baked Kale Chips (page 20)

EAT IT AT HOME WITH:
a fried egg on top and tomato wedges dressed with Mustard Vinaigrette (page 162)

MAKE IT A PARTY WITH:
Simple Green Salad (page 180) and chilled rosé

Sausage & Escarole with White Beans

SERVES 4 TO 6

I spent some of my college years in Rochester, New York, attending art school at RIT's School for American Crafts. (Isn't that what most chefs do before they get into the kitchen?) One of the main culinary forces in Rochester is the population with roots in central Italy, and this was a signature dish on the menus of most of the Italian restaurants in town. If you can find butcher-made Italian sausage, grab it.

1 pound Italian sausage (about 4 sausages), sweet or hot

2 tablespoons extra-virgin olive oil, as needed

4 cloves garlic, minced

¼ teaspoon crushed dried red pepper

1 head escarole, leaves chopped into 2-inch pieces

Two 15-ounce cans cannellini beans, drained but not rinsed

3 cups chicken stock (page 118)

2 tablespoons unsalted butter

2 tablespoons chopped fresh flat-leaf parsley

½ cup freshly grated Parmesan cheese, plus more for sprinkling

2 plum tomatoes, diced

Salt and freshly ground black pepper to taste

Crusty bread, for serving

PACK IT TO GO WITH:
baguette slices

EAT IT AT HOME WITH:
Roasted Eggplant Spread (page 49) on crostini

MAKE IT A PARTY WITH:
arugula tossed with Mustard Vinaigrette (page 162) and toasted Italian bread brushed with garlic and olive oil

Remove the sausage from its casings and break it into 1-inch chunks. Cook the sausage pieces in a large skillet over medium heat until they brown on all sides, about 10 minutes. If the pan doesn't have any rendered fat or oil from the sausage, add the olive oil. Add the garlic and crushed red pepper to the skillet and cook, stirring, just until the garlic softens and becomes slightly golden, about 1 minute. Add the escarole and cook, stirring, until wilted, 2 to 3 minutes. Add the beans and cook, stirring, for 1 minute. Add the stock, bring to a gentle boil, and keep at a gentle boil for 5 minutes. Add the butter, parsley, cheese, and tomatoes. Stir to combine, then cook until the mixture is heated through and the butter has melted. Taste, then add the salt and pepper, if needed (different brands of sausage have different levels of salt and pepper, so this might vary), and then taste again. Adjust the seasoning if needed. Serve in bowls with crusty bread on the side to dip in the juice. This keeps in an airtight container in the refrigerator for up to 5 days.

Main Course Salads

Slow-Roasted Salmon Niçoise Salad

Smoked Salmon Caesar Salad

Grilled Beef Tenderloin & Baked Potato Salad

Cobb Salad with Blue Cheese Vinaigrette

Burrata with Grape Tomato & Celery Salad

Chicken Salad 101

Slow-Roasted Salmon Niçoise Salad

SERVES 4

I love cooking salmon this way, slowly and at a low temperature. It's so easy, and gives the salmon a melt-in-your-mouth texture. My uncle Robert and aunt Greta are inspirational cooks and hosts, and they served me this salmon one time in their posh Manhattan apartment. The next day, I insisted they teach me how to make it, and now I make it about twice a month, whenever I need to make a luncheon main course. Although tuna is the traditional fish in a Niçoise salad, this salmon is so delicious that I much prefer this version.

FOR THE SALMON
One 1-pound Icelandic or other salmon fillet, skinned and deboned
Salt and freshly ground black pepper

FOR THE SALAD
4 cups torn romaine lettuce leaves
4 cups chopped iceberg lettuce
½ cup Mustard Vinaigrette (page 162)

2 medium red potatoes, boiled, cubed, and chilled
1 cup green beans, blanched and cut into 1-inch pieces
4 hard-boiled large eggs (see page 88), sliced
16 pitted kalamata or other cured olives
24 cherry tomatoes, halved

PACK IT TO GO WITH:
baguette slices

EAT IT AT HOME WITH:
sea salt crackers and Iced Tea (page 245) with a lemon wedge

MAKE IT A PARTY WITH:
Prosecco and Madeleines (page 219)

Heat the oven to 225 degrees.

Make the salmon: Line a baking sheet with foil. Place the salmon fillet on the foil and sprinkle the fillet evenly with salt and pepper. Bake for 15 to 20 minutes, until the salmon is cooked through but still very soft, bright in color, and tender. Let cool on the pan for 20 minutes, then cover the pan and refrigerate until ready to use, or for up to 3 days.

Make the salad: In a bowl, combine the romaine and iceberg lettuces and toss them with the vinaigrette. Distribute the dressed lettuce evenly among 4 plates, placing it in the center of each. Dividing the ingredients evenly among the plates, make piles of the potatoes, green beans, eggs, olives, and tomatoes around the edge of the lettuce. Break the chilled salmon into pieces and divide them evenly among the 4 plates, placing them in a pile on top of the lettuce. (If you're making this to go, you can quarter the recipe and pack the ingredients together in an airtight container.)

Mustard Vinaigrette

MAKES ABOUT ½ CUP

1 teaspoon Dijon mustard

3 tablespoons red wine vinegar

6 tablespoons extra-virgin olive oil

Salt and freshly ground black pepper

My kitchen comrade Dorie Greenspan (author of Baking with Julia, *in which I was included, and other great pastry books) writes eloquently about making her mustard vinaigrette right in the Dijon mustard jar. Once the jar is what most would consider empty, Dorie shakes up the perfect mustard vinaigrette, knowing there's just enough mustard clinging to the walls of the jar. But even if you don't have a nearly empty jar of Dijon mustard, here's how to make a batch of vinaigrette. And feel free to double it so you have enough for more than one salad.*

Place the mustard, vinegar, olive oil, and salt and pepper to taste in a jar with a lid. Screw the lid on the jar and shake the jar vigorously to combine and emulsify the dressing. Taste to see if you need more salt or pepper. The vinaigrette keeps in the jar or another airtight container in the refrigerator for up to 1 month.

Burrata with Grape Tomato & Celery Salad

SERVES 4

One of my favorite cheeses is a creamy-centered mozzarella called burrata. It used to be almost impossible to find, so I would venture to Di Palo's on Grand Street in New York City's Little Italy to get it. And they only had it on Wednesdays, the day it arrived from Rome. Now you can get it almost anywhere, and I am a happier chef for that.

4 fresh basil leaves, torn into ½-inch pieces

2 teaspoons chopped fresh flat-leaf parsley

¼ cup extra-virgin olive oil

2 tablespoons red wine vinegar

Salt and freshly ground black pepper

24 grape tomatoes, halved

1 stalk celery, thinly sliced crosswise

One 8-ounce ball burrata cheese

In a medium bowl, combine the basil, parsley, olive oil, vinegar, salt, and pepper and mix with a fork to combine. Add the tomatoes and celery and toss to coat. Cut the ball of burrata in quarters and place each quarter on a plate. Spoon the tomato mixture over the burrata, making sure to drizzle some of the dressing left in the bowl over the burrata too. Serve immediately.

PACK IT TO GO WITH:
slices of Italian spiced ham rolled and secured with a toothpick

EAT IT AT HOME WITH:
thinly sliced prosciutto and Italian bread

MAKE IT A PARTY WITH:
Gemelli with Peas and Pancetta (page 135) and your favorite biscotti

Smoked Salmon Caesar Salad

SERVES 1

Whenever I spot a Caesar salad on a menu, I order it. I've tried it in restaurants all over the country, searching for greatness. In the tastiest versions, I love the crunch of the lettuce and the creaminess of the dressing, with its bright lemon and salty anchovy flavors. (I think pureed anchovy fillets give the best flavor; anchovy paste works too.) The addition of smoked salmon, hard-boiled egg, blanched green beans, and crispy radishes makes a hearty main course salad. You can use store-bought dressing, but in case you want to make your own, I've included my favorite recipe for it, which I've developed over the years at my various restaurants.

¼ head romaine lettuce, washed and torn into 1½-inch pieces

6 cherry tomatoes, halved

1 cup 1-inch blanched green bean pieces

¼ cup sliced radishes

About ¼ cup Caesar Dressing (recipe opposite)

3 ounces sliced smoked salmon

1 hard-boiled large egg (see page 88), cut lengthwise into sixths

6 to 8 Parmesan shards (shaved off a large block with a vegetable peeler)

¼ cup Caesar croutons (your favorite prepared version)

½ teaspoon snipped fresh chives (optional)

PACK IT TO GO WITH:
green grapes

EAT IT AT HOME WITH:
a glass of Sauvignon Blanc

MAKE IT A PARTY WITH:
warmed multigrain rolls spread with unsalted butter and sprinkled with snipped chives, and Pastel Fruit Salad (page 230)

In a large bowl, combine the lettuce, tomatoes, green beans, and radishes and toss with the dressing. Place in a serving bowl, then garnish with the salmon, egg, Parmesan, croutons, and chives, if using. Serve immediately.

Caesar Dressing

MAKES ABOUT 1¼ CUPS

This dressing contains a raw egg yolk, so please use organic eggs from a reliable source, keep your eggs refrigerated, and don't serve this to anyone who has a compromised immune system.

Use a blender or a whisk to combine the mustard, lemon juice, vinegar, Worcestershire sauce, anchovies (mash them first if whisking by hand), and pepper. Blend well, then add the egg yolk and blend until emulsified. With the blender running or while whisking, pour the olive oil into the mixture in a thin stream until emulsified. Add the Parmesan and blend just until combined. Use immediately or refrigerate in an airtight container for up to 1 week.

1 tablespoon Dijon mustard

1 tablespoon freshly squeezed lemon juice

2 tablespoons red wine vinegar

1 teaspoon Worcestershire sauce

2 anchovy fillets, or 1 teaspoon anchovy paste

½ teaspoon freshly ground black pepper

1 large egg yolk

½ cup extra-virgin olive oil

½ cup freshly grated Parmesan cheese

Grilled Beef Tenderloin & Baked Potato Salad

SERVES 1

Here's a somewhat lighter—yet still satisfying—version of steak and potatoes, with beef tenderloin and potatoes as elements of a hearty salad. You can fire up your grill and get all the cooking done at once. I keep my grill on my screened porch so I can grill year-round.

3 ounces beef tenderloin

Salt and freshly ground black pepper

1 small baked potato, cut into ³/₈-inch thick slices

2 rings green bell pepper, cut into ³/₈-inch thick slices

1 small tomato, halved horizontally

2 teaspoons extra-virgin olive oil

2 cups chopped romaine lettuce

2 cups coarsely chopped iceberg lettuce

1 hard-boiled large egg (see page 88), quartered

¹/₄ cup prepared creamy ranch dressing

Heat your grill to medium or medium-high (if you prefer your beef rare, heat it to medium-high; if you prefer it medium-rare or medium, heat the grill to medium so the outside doesn't cook too much before the inside reaches your desired doneness).

Season the tenderloin well with salt and pepper. Place it on the grill and grill it on all sides to the doneness you desire; cooking times will vary. (For medium-rare, grill the tenderloin for almost 6 minutes per side.) Remove from the grill and let rest until you assemble the salad.

Brush the cut faces of the baked potato slices, pepper rings, and tomato halves with olive oil and sprinkle them with salt and pepper. Grill them over medium heat until they have grill marks on them, 6 to 8 minutes for the potato slices and 4 to 5 minutes for the pepper rings and tomato halves. (Grill the potato slices and pepper rings on both sides to get grill marks, but the tomato on only one side.) Once marked, let them rest at room temperature until cooled, about 15 minutes. Cut the pepper rings into 1-inch pieces and cut the tomato into chunks.

In a salad bowl, toss the romaine and iceberg lettuces together. Slice the tenderloin into ¹/₄-inch-thick slices and tuck them into the lettuce, along with the potato, bell pepper, tomato, and egg. Stir ¹/₂ teaspoon freshly ground black pepper into the ranch dressing. Drizzle the salad with the dressing and serve. (If you're taking this to go, pack the dressing separately.)

PACK IT TO GO WITH: *pumpernickel crackers*

EAT IT AT HOME WITH: *grilled Tuscan bread—brush the surface of the bread with extra-virgin olive oil and grill it along with the potatoes and tomatoes*

MAKE IT A PARTY WITH: *Potato Leek Soup (page 106) and Orange-Scented Chocolate Brownies (page 214)*

Cobb Salad with Blue Cheese Vinaigrette

SERVES 1

As one version of the story goes, Robert Cobb invented the Cobb salad in 1937 at the famous Brown Derby restaurant in L.A. He needed to make a late-night snack for Sid Grauman, the great showman and owner of Grauman's Chinese Theater. The cooks had gone home, so Cobb used whatever leftover prepared ingredients he could find. The Brown Derby was a hangout for many of the biggest stars of the day, and word spread quickly about this particular salad, which has since become an American classic.

2 cups chopped romaine lettuce

2 cups chopped Boston lettuce

¼ cup frozen or canned corn kernels

4 ounces grilled chicken, torn into big chunks

2 strips cooked bacon, cut into ¼-inch pieces

6 cherry tomatoes, halved

1 hard-boiled large egg (see page 88), coarsely chopped

2 white button mushrooms, sliced

½ cup cubed seedless (English) cucumber

¼ ripe avocado, pitted, peeled, and cubed

¼ cup Blue Cheese Vinaigrette (page 169)

PACK IT TO GO WITH:
a sourdough roll

EAT IT AT HOME WITH:
sliced pears

MAKE IT A PARTY WITH:
Dates with Goat Cheese (page 38) and Roasted Rosemary Cashews (page 24)

Place the romaine and Boston lettuces in a low, flat salad bowl. Line up the corn, chicken, bacon, tomatoes, egg, mushrooms, cucumber, and avocado in rows on top of the lettuces. Drizzle the vinaigrette over the salad, and serve. (If you're taking this to go, pack the dressing separately.)

Blue Cheese Vinaigrette

MAKES ABOUT 1 CUP

In a small bowl, whisk together the vinegar, mustard, honey, salt, and pepper. Slowly whisk in the olive oil until emulsified. Add the blue cheese and stir gently to combine. The dressing keeps in an airtight container in the refrigerator for up to 2 weeks.

¹⁄₄ cup red wine vinegar

2 teaspoons Dijon mustard

1 teaspoon honey

¹⁄₄ teaspoon salt

3 grinds black pepper

¹⁄₂ cup extra-virgin olive oil

¹⁄₄ cup crumbled Roquefort or other blue cheese

Chicken Salad 101

Chicken salad is always a crowd-pleaser, whether you put it on a sandwich, in a pita pocket, in a wrap, on top of salad greens, or in a bowl with crackers on the side. It's also versatile: You can use almost any kind of cooked chicken meat (I give instructions for roasting and poaching here) and play with the other ingredients, whether they're crunchy vegetables like water chestnuts or fennel; chewy dried fruits like apricots, pineapple, or raisins; light herbs like parsley, dill, or tarragon; or other crunchy elements like toasted nuts or sesame seeds. This section includes a few of my tried-and-true ways to make chicken salad, and I hope you'll use these recipes as a jumping-off point for developing new favorites.

Simple Roasted Chicken

SERVES 4

Sometimes I just need to roast a chicken. Maybe it's for lunch or dinner, or for chicken salad, or for chicken and dumplings, or to make my kids yell, "What's that good smell?" when they walk in after school. Having a chicken roasting in the oven makes me feel that all is right with the world, for the moment. How can such a basic act of cooking do all this? Try it. You'll see.

1 whole roasting chicken (about 4½ pounds)

Salt and freshly ground black pepper

1 small carrot, peeled and cut crosswise into 1-inch pieces

1 small stalk celery, with its top, cut crosswise into 1-inch pieces

1 small onion, peeled and cut into quarters

1 bay leaf, broken up into 4 pieces

3 sprigs fresh thyme, or ½ teaspoon dried thyme

3 cloves garlic, halved

½ lemon, cut into ¼-inch-thick slices

3 sprigs fresh flat-leaf parsley, including the stems, cut into 1-inch segments

Heat the oven to 400 degrees.

Rinse the chicken inside and out with cold water and place it in a roasting pan. Season the inside of the chicken well with salt and pepper.

Place the carrot, celery, onion, bay leaf, thyme, garlic, lemon slices, and parsley in a bowl and toss them together to combine. Stuff the mixture into the cavity of the chicken. If the chicken is completely stuffed and you have some of the mixture left over, add it to the bottom of the roasting pan and place the chicken on top of it. Sprinkle the outside of the stuffed chicken generously with salt and pepper. Roast the chicken until the juices in the thigh run clear when pierced, 1¼ to 1½ hours. Remove from the oven and let the chicken rest for 5 minutes, then carve and serve, or let the chicken cool and pull the meat off the bones as needed. The roasted chicken keeps, covered, in the refrigerator for up to 5 days.

Poached Chicken Breasts

MAKES 2 BREASTS

This is an easy way to cook chicken breasts. Sometimes I want only milder-flavored white meat for my chicken salad, so I use these. After you've poached the chicken, you can shred or slice the meat for myriad uses. You can toss it with salad greens, combine it with green apples, red onion, celery, and mayo for a salad, add it to a soup, or toss it into an Asian-inspired pasta dish, such as Copperwell Noodles (page 136).

Two 6- to 8-ounce chicken breasts
1 bay leaf
6 whole black peppercorns
1 small carrot, thickly sliced

½ stalk celery or celery tops, thickly sliced
1 large sprig fresh flat-leaf parsley
1 sprig fresh thyme
4 cups chicken stock (page 112)

Heat the oven to 325 degrees.

Place the chicken breasts in a shallow roasting pan, then add the bay leaf, peppercorns, carrot, celery, parsley, thyme, and chicken stock. Bake (uncovered) for 30 to 35 minutes, depending on the size of the breasts. The meat should be white in the center and register 165 degrees on a meat thermometer. Let the chicken cool for 10 minutes in the liquid, then transfer it to a plate to finish cooling. Strain the poaching liquid (chicken stock), then chill it or freeze it to use in soup, risotto, or sauces. Use the chicken immediately or store in an airtight container in the refrigerator for up to 4 days.

Classic Chicken Salad

MAKES ABOUT 4 CUPS

Here's a classic chicken salad with celery for crunch and a mix of mayo and Greek yogurt for a lighter, tangy binding.

¼ cup mayonnaise

¼ cup Greek yogurt

1 teaspoon spicy mustard

1 tablespoon chopped fresh flat-leaf parsley

2 finely chopped poached chicken breasts (see opposite)

1 stalk celery, diced

Salt, as needed

In a medium bowl, combine the mayonnaise, yogurt, mustard, and parsley. Add the chicken and celery and mix with a fork to combine. Taste and season with salt, if needed. Serve immediately or store in an airtight container in the refrigerator for up to 3 days.

Teriyaki Chicken Salad

Last fall, I cooked in Thailand for the World Gourmet Festival, and one of my rewards for doing that was a stay at one of the world's finest hotels, the Four Seasons in Chiang Mai. This chicken salad is available on the poolside menu there. It was so good I asked the chef how to make it. It's memorable but surprisingly simple.

¼ cup mayonnaise

¼ cup teriyaki sauce

2 cups shredded or chopped roasted chicken (see page 171)

One 8-ounce can sliced water chestnuts, drained and roughly chopped

1 scallion, sliced

Pita bread, for serving (optional)

Belgian endive leaves, for serving (optional)

In a bowl, stir together the mayonnaise and teriyaki sauce until blended. Add the chicken, water chestnuts, and scallion and toss to combine. Stuff the salad into pita halves or serve with Belgian endive leaves for scooping. I like to use this salad immediately, but you can keep it in an airtight container in the refrigerator for up to 1 day.

Mexican Chicken Salad

MAKES ABOUT 4 CUPS

This chicken salad is great in a wrap, on crackers, with corn chips for dipping, or on a bed of butter lettuce with a crusty roll. Cumin, cilantro, and chiles (if you want them) give it Mexican flavor and flair.

$\frac{1}{3}$ cup sour cream

$\frac{1}{3}$ cup mayonnaise

3 tablespoons freshly squeezed lime juice

2 tablespoons tomato salsa (store-bought, or see page 45; you choose mild, medium, or hot)

2 tablespoons minced fresh cilantro

1 tablespoon minced canned green chiles (optional)

$\frac{1}{2}$ teaspoon salt

$\frac{1}{4}$ teaspoon freshly ground black pepper

$\frac{1}{4}$ teaspoon ground cumin

2 cups diced roasted chicken (see page 171)

$\frac{2}{3}$ cup canned black beans, drained

$\frac{1}{3}$ cup diced red bell pepper

$\frac{1}{3}$ cup frozen or canned corn kernels

1 scallion, thinly sliced

$\frac{1}{2}$ avocado, pitted, peeled, and cubed

In a bowl, stir together the sour cream, mayonnaise, lime juice, salsa, cilantro, chiles (if using), salt, pepper, and cumin. Add the chicken, black beans, bell pepper, corn, and scallion and gently fold them into the sour cream mixture with a rubber spatula. Add the avocado and gently fold it into the mixture. Cover the bowl and chill for at least 30 minutes before serving, or store in an airtight container in the refrigerator for up to 3 days.

Chicken Salad with Dried Cranberries, Fennel, & Toasted Almonds

Chicken salad can be made in about a million different ways. No matter how I make it, I always include something crunchy, whether it's the typical chopped celery or something a little different. In this version, the crunch comes from fennel and almonds. Tart dried cranberries add punch, but feel free to try another dried fruit, such as dried cherries or chopped dried apricots.

4 cups chopped roasted chicken (about the amount from a whole chicken; see page 171)

¼ cup dried cranberries

¼ cup diced fennel bulb

¼ cup sliced almonds, toasted (see Note, page 26)

½ cup mayonnaise

1 tablespoon freshly squeezed lemon juice

1 teaspoon chopped fresh flat-leaf parsley

⅛ teaspoon freshly ground black pepper

Place the chicken, cranberries, fennel, almonds, mayonnaise, lemon juice, parsley, and pepper in a medium bowl and stir with a fork until well combined. Use in a sandwich or on some mixed greens for a nice lunch salad, or store in an airtight container in the refrigerator for up to 5 days.

Vegetable Salads & Sides

Simple Green Salad

Three-Beet Salad with Snap Peas

Roasted Beets and Carrots with Orange

Kale Salad with Pine Nuts,
Raisins, & Parmesan

Garden Vegetable Coleslaw

Roasted Cauliflower

Vinaigrette Potato Salad

Loaded Potato Salad

Herbed Spaghetti Squash with Crispy Pancetta

Delicata Squash with Garlic

Maple Sweet Potato Puree with Hazelnuts

Roasted Vegetable Salad

Roasted Asparagus with Walnuts
& Goat Cheese

Roasted Pumpkin with Scallion,
Rosemary, & Raisins

Simple Green Salad

SERVES 4

When you're wondering what to make for lunch, don't forget how perfect a simple green salad can be. It pairs well with so many things, from soup to more substantial main courses. It acts as a palate cleanser, and it offers lots of contrasting textures. You may already have a favorite version of a green salad; here's mine.

1 cup snap peas, blanched

½ avocado, pitted, peeled, and cubed

2 jarred artichoke hearts, chopped

1 small head Boston or butter lettuce, washed and dried, leaves torn into 2-inch pieces

One 2-inch segment seedless (English) cucumber, halved lengthwise and cut into half-moons

1 head Belgian endive, leaves sliced at an angle into ½-inch strips

¼ cup fresh flat-leaf parsley leaves

¼ cup Mustard Vinaigrette (page 162)

1 pinch salt

1 pinch freshly ground black pepper

Place the snap peas, avocado, artichoke hearts, lettuce, cucumber, endive, and parsley in a bowl and toss to combine. Drizzle with vinaigrette, season with the salt and pepper, toss one more time, and serve.

Three-Beet Salad with Snap Peas

SERVES 4

Any mix of beets will work for this recipe, so I suggest going to the farmers' market and seeing what they have to play with. That's what I do. I'm a big fan of seeing what's available and letting the garden gods decide what I'm making.

FOR THE SALAD
1 medium red beet
1 medium golden beet
1 medium zebra-striped beet
½ pound snap peas, blanched

FOR THE DRESSING
¼ cup extra-virgin olive oil
2 tablespoons balsamic vinegar
¼ teaspoon salt
⅛ teaspoon freshly ground black pepper
1 tablespoon chopped fresh flat-leaf
   parsley

Heat the oven to 400 degrees.

Trim off the tops of the beets and wash the beets (reserve the tops for another use, such as Farro with Beet Greens, Leeks, & Garlic on page 122, or discard them). Place the beets on a sheet of foil and gather up the foil to enclose them completely. Place the foil-wrapped beets on a baking sheet and roast for 1 hour, until tender. Remove the beets from the oven and let them cool slightly, about 5 minutes, before unwrapping them. (Oil your hands before peeling beets if you want to keep your hands from turning red.) Peel the beets by rubbing the skins off (they will come off in big pieces). Cut the beets into 1½-inch chunks and set aside in a bowl.

Cut the snap peas in half so the pieces are about 1 inch long.

Add the olive oil, vinegar, salt, and pepper to the bowl with the beets and toss to coat, then tuck in the snap peas and sprinkle with the parsley. Give the salad one light toss (if you toss the peas too much with the balsamic and beets, they will lose their bright green color) and serve. This salad keeps in an airtight container in the refrigerator for up to 3 days, but the peas will lose their bright green color after 1 day.

Roasted Beets & Carrots
with Orange

SERVES 4 TO 6

I have worked at a historical farm in Lake Forest, about 15 minutes from my house, cooking and baking for their farmers' market. One weekend we held a garden symposium, and I spoke about farm-to-table cooking and then served everyone a buffet lunch in the kitchen. The dishes were simple and fresh, and everyone loved what we made—especially this mix of roasted beets and orange-glazed carrots.

8 medium red, golden, or striped beets

6 medium carrots, peeled

2 tablespoons extra-virgin olive oil

Salt and freshly ground black pepper

½ cup freshly squeezed orange juice

1 teaspoon grated orange zest

1 tablespoon chopped fresh flat-leaf parsley

Heat the oven to 400 degrees.

Trim off the tops of the beets and wash the beets (reserve the tops for another use, or discard them). Place the beets on a sheet of foil and gather up the foil to enclose them completely. Place the foil-wrapped beets on a baking sheet and roast for 1 hour, until tender. Remove the beets from the oven and let them cool slightly, about 5 minutes, before unwrapping them. (Oil your hands before peeling beets if you want to keep your hands from turning red.) Peel the beets by rubbing the skins off (they will come off in big pieces). Cut the beets up into big chunks and set them aside in a bowl.

While the beets are in the oven, cut the carrots into chunks (I use a Japanese roll cut here; see Note, page 205), place them in a roasting pan, drizzle them with the olive oil, and season with salt and pepper to taste. Roast the carrots until tender, 20 to 30 minutes. Pour the orange juice into the pan and continue roasting for another 15 minutes to reduce the liquid and glaze the carrots.

Add the roasted carrots to the bowl with the beets, add the orange zest, and gently combine them. Sprinkle with the parsley, and serve. This dish keeps in an airtight container in the refrigerator for 2 to 3 days, but the color of the beets will start to bleed into everything.

Kale Salad with Pine Nuts, Raisins, & Parmesan

SERVES 4

Kale has become one of my favorite vegetables. It's delicious sautéed with garlic as a side dish, rubbed with oil, salt, and pepper and baked for a crunchy snack, or thinly sliced and served in this addictive salad. And it's loaded with vitamins! Flatter leaf varieties work better for this salad (instead of the curly leaf type). My preferred variety is called dinosaur (or lacinto) kale; ask for that or something like it at the farmers' market.

12 large kale leaves

¼ cup extra-virgin olive oil

2 tablespoons freshly squeezed lemon juice

¼ cup pine nuts, toasted (see Note, page 26)

¼ cup raisins

Salt and freshly ground black pepper

¼ cup coarsely grated Parmesan cheese

Cut the spines out of the kale leaves and stack the leaves flat, one on top of the other, on a cutting board. Roll the leaves tightly, then slice them crosswise into very thin strips, about ⅛ to ¼ inch wide (this method is called chiffonade). Place the kale strips in a large mixing bowl and add the olive oil, lemon juice, pine nuts, raisins, and salt and pepper to taste. Toss very well to coat the kale; the kale should look dark and shiny. Sprinkle with the Parmesan and serve immediately, or refrigerate in an airtight container for up to 3 days.

Garden Vegetable Coleslaw

SERVES 4

Although coleslaw is typically made from shredded cabbage, you can make variations on coleslaw from all kinds of vegetables, as long as they're firm enough to shred or grate. When I created this version, I thought about flavor and color, and the result is a bright and tasty mix.

1 zucchini, ends trimmed

1 broccoli stem

2 medium golden beets, peeled

2 medium carrots, peeled

1 small celery root, peeled and quartered

¼ cup cider vinegar

1 teaspoon salt

1 teaspoon Dijon mustard

1 teaspoon sugar

¼ teaspoon freshly ground black pepper

½ cup extra-virgin olive oil

2 tablespoons roughly chopped fresh cilantro leaves

½ cup fresh flat-leaf parsley leaves

Using a food processor fitted with the grater blade, shred the zucchini, broccoli, beets, carrots, and celery root. (You may need to cut the vegetables into chunks to fit into the food processor; it depends on the size of your food processor's opening. Alternatively, shred the vegetables by hand on the large holes of a box grater.) Place the shredded vegetables in a large bowl.

In a small bowl, whisk together the vinegar, salt, mustard, sugar, and pepper. While whisking, drizzle in the olive oil to emulsify. Pour the dressing over the shredded vegetables, add the cilantro and parsley, and toss until well combined. Cover and chill for at least 20 minutes before serving to let the vegetables absorb the flavors of the dressing. The coleslaw keeps in an airtight container in the refrigerator for up to 3 days.

Roasted Cauliflower

SERVES 4

When you roast cauliflower this way it almost tastes sweet. It's addictive—once I start eating it, it's hard to stop, whether it's hot out of the oven or cold and left over from the day before. It's on a lot of my last-minute lunch menus, and friends often ask for the recipe. So here it is!

1 head cauliflower

2 tablespoons extra-virgin olive oil

1 teaspoon salt

¼ teaspoon freshly ground black pepper

1 clove garlic, minced

1 tablespoon chopped fresh flat-leaf parsley

Heat the oven to 400 degrees.

Cut the core out of the head of cauliflower and remove the leaves. Break the florets apart. Cut any larger florets into smaller pieces.

In a shallow roasting pan, toss the cauliflower with the olive oil, salt, pepper, and garlic. Roast for 25 to 30 minutes, until the cauliflower is tender, cooked through, and starting to brown. Divide the cauliflower evenly among 4 plates, sprinkle with the parsley, and serve. The cauliflower keeps in an airtight container in the refrigerator for up to 3 days.

Vinaigrette Potato Salad

SERVES 4 TO 6

For picnics and on-the-go lunches I prefer a potato salad made with vinaigrette to one made with mayo because mayonnaise and the warm outdoors don't mix so well. This one is rich with flavor from the bacon and chives.

2 pounds red potatoes washed but not peeled, and halved (quartered if large)

6 strips bacon, sliced into ¼-inch strips

2 shallots or 1 small onion, chopped

1 clove garlic, minced

2 tablespoons coarse-grain mustard

6 tablespoons cider vinegar

1 tablespoon honey

½ teaspoon celery seed

1 teaspoon salt

½ teaspoon freshly ground black pepper

2 tablespoons snipped fresh chives

2 tablespoons chopped fresh flat-leaf parsley

Place the potatoes in a large pot with enough water to cover them. Bring the water to a boil over high heat, then reduce the heat to medium and simmer until the potatoes are fork tender, 15 to 20 minutes. (Don't overcook them or they could fall apart.) Drain the potatoes in a colander and set aside to cool.

In a skillet, cook the sliced bacon over medium heat until almost crisp, about 5 minutes. Add the shallots and cook, stirring, for 3 minutes more, until the shallots are almost translucent. Add the garlic and cook for 1 minute more. Turn off the heat and whisk in the mustard, vinegar, honey, celery seed, salt, and pepper. Pour the vinaigrette over the slightly cooled potatoes and gently fold and toss them to coat. Mix in the chives and parsley and serve warm or at room temperature. The potato salad keeps in an airtight container in the refrigerator for up to 3 days.

Loaded Potato Salad

SERVES 4 TO 6

This rivals the best potato salads I've ever tasted. It combines classic potato salad with the best parts of a loaded potato skin: scallion, cheese, sour cream, and bacon.

2 pounds russet potatoes, peeled and halved (or quartered, if large)

½ pound bacon, cooked, cooled, and diced

¼ cup sliced scallions

1 clove garlic, minced

1 cup shredded sharp cheddar cheese

1 cup mayonnaise

½ cup sour cream or plain yogurt

1 teaspoon snipped fresh chives

½ teaspoon salt

½ teaspoon freshly ground black pepper

Place the potatoes in a large pot with enough water to cover them. Bring the water to a boil over high heat, then reduce the heat to medium and simmer until the potatoes are fork tender, 15 to 20 minutes. (Don't overcook them or they could fall apart.) Drain the potatoes in a colander and set aside to cool.

In a medium bowl, combine the bacon, scallions, garlic, cheese, mayonnaise, sour cream, chives, salt, and pepper and fold them with a rubber spatula to combine. When the potatoes have cooled, cut them into 1-inch cubes and add them to the mayonnaise mixture, folding them in gently to coat. Serve immediately, or chill for 2 hours to help the flavors develop before serving. The potato salad keeps in an airtight container in the refrigerator for up to 4 days.

Herbed Spaghetti Squash
with Crispy Pancetta

SERVES 4 TO 6

In the fall when squash is in season, plentiful, and cheap, I like to make all kinds of squash dishes. I use buttercup, acorn, butternut, pumpkin, delicata, and spaghetti squash. Spaghetti squash has texture like no other, with natural strands of tender flesh that really do seem like spaghetti. Its delicate flavor shows off whatever herbs you use, so subtlety is key. This recipe's so simple because most of the cooking is done in the oven, with a quick finish on the stove. It reheats beautifully (if you don't finish it the first round).

1 medium spaghetti squash

Salt and freshly ground black pepper

¼ pound sliced pancetta, julienned

2 tablespoons unsalted butter

3 tablespoons chopped mixed fresh herbs (chervil, tarragon, dill, parsley, basil, and chives)

Heat the oven to 400 degrees.

Cut the squash in half lengthwise and sprinkle the cut surfaces with salt and pepper. Place the squash, cut sides down, on a baking sheet and roast for 45 minutes.

Meanwhile, heat a sauté pan over medium heat. Add the pancetta and cook, stirring, until crispy, 5 to 10 minutes. Using a slotted spoon, remove the pancetta from the pan and set it aside in a bowl; leave the fat in the pan.

Remove the squash from the oven and let it cool for 10 minutes, then use a fork to dig the strands of flesh away from the skin. Set aside.

In the sauté pan with the reserved pancetta fat, melt the butter over medium heat. Add the spaghetti squash strands, the chervil, tarragon, dill, parsley, basil, and chives and toss to combine and heat through. Taste and season with salt and pepper, if needed. Place the squash in a serving dish and sprinkle it with the crispy pancetta. This dish keeps in an airtight container in the refrigerator for up to 4 days.

Delicata Squash with Garlic

SERVES 4

Delicata is a beautifully striped oblong squash with skin so tender there's no need to peel it before cooking and eating it. Just slice it into rings, clean out the seeds, season it, give it some time in the oven, and you have the flavor of fall on a plate. Vanilla beans are an unexpected addition to this savory dish, but they add welcome subtle sweetness and dimension to this simple preparation.

2 delicata squash

2 tablespoons extra-virgin olive oil

1 teaspoon salt

¼ teaspoon freshly ground black pepper

2 cloves garlic, minced

1 vanilla bean, split then cut in half

Heat the oven to 400 degrees.

Slice the squash into rings and seed them. Place the rings on a baking sheet in slightly overlapping rows. Drizzle with the olive oil, then sprinkle with the salt and pepper. Scatter the minced garlic evenly over the squash, then lay the 4 vanilla bean pieces on top. Bake for about 35 minutes, until tender. Serve hot. The squash keeps in an airtight container in the refrigerator for up to 4 days.

Maple Sweet Potato Puree with Hazelnuts

SERVES 6

The puree part of this is easy to make in advance, and you can omit the sautéed shallots to save time. The puree reheats beautifully, and tastes good cold too!

4 large sweet potatoes (about 2½ pounds)

2 tablespoons Greek yogurt

2 tablespoons unsalted butter, at room temperature

2 tablespoons pure maple syrup

Salt and freshly ground black pepper

1 small shallot, peeled and sliced

¼ cup chopped hazelnuts, toasted (see Note, page 26)

Heat the oven to 400 degrees.

Rinse the potatoes and pierce them with a fork in a few places to allow steam to vent. Place them on a baking sheet and roast for 50 to 60 minutes, until completely soft. Let cool.

When the potatoes are cool enough to handle, cut them in half and scoop the flesh into the bowl of a food processor. Add the yogurt, 1 tablespoon of the butter, and the maple syrup and pulse until the mixture is smooth. Season to taste with salt and pepper. Transfer the mixture to a covered casserole and keep warm until ready to serve, or cover and refrigerate for up to 3 days.

Heat the remaining 1 tablespoon butter in a small sauté pan and add the shallot. Cook, stirring, until the shallot is translucent, about 4 minutes. Add the hazelnuts and heat them through. Spoon the shallot and hazelnuts over the sweet potato puree just before serving. The puree keeps, covered, in the refrigerator for up to 3 days.

Roasted Vegetable Salad

SERVES 4 TO 6

This Mediterranean-inspired salad is more like a chilled ratatouille, but it's cold and full of vegetables, so I call it a salad. Roasting is a nice way to tenderize veggies and concentrate their flavors, bringing out the natural sweetness that's hiding when you eat them raw. Throw some balls of mozzarella on top and you have a main course, a great chunky pasta sauce, or a topping for couscous.

FOR THE ROASTED VEGETABLES

½ cup extra-virgin olive oil

1 zucchini, halved lengthwise

1 yellow squash, halved lengthwise

10 spears asparagus, woody ends trimmed

½ yellow bell pepper, sliced crosswise into rings

1 Japanese eggplant, cut lengthwise into ¼-inch-thick strips

1 medium red onion, sliced into rings

6 baby portobello mushrooms, halved

2 plum tomatoes, quartered lengthwise

2 garlic cloves, peeled and minced

¼ teaspoon fresh or dried thyme

¼ teaspoon dried oregano

1 teaspoon salt

¼ teaspoon freshly ground black pepper

FOR THE DRESSING

¼ cup extra-virgin olive oil

2 tablespoons red wine vinegar

1 tablespoon chopped capers

2 teaspoons snipped fresh chives

Salt

¼ cup pitted black olives, oil cured if possible, halved

Block Parmesan cheese, for shaving

Make the vegetables: Heat the oven to 400 degrees.

Oil two baking sheets well with some of the olive oil and place the zucchini, yellow squash, asparagus, and bell pepper on one and the eggplant, onion, mushrooms, and tomatoes on the other. (The veggies on the second sheet may need a little extra time in the oven.) Make sure the vegetables are lying flat in a single layer. Drizzle them with the remaining olive oil, then sprinkle them evenly with the garlic, thyme, oregano, salt, and pepper. Roast the vegetables for 20 to 25 minutes, until cooked through. Let the vegetables cool on the pans, then cover the pans and chill the vegetables until ready to use, or for up to 2 days.

> **" Roasting is a nice way to tenderize veggies and concentrate their flavors, bringing out the natural sweetness . . . "**

Make the dressing: Whisk together the olive oil, vinegar, capers, chives, and salt to taste.

Once the vegetables have cooled completely, cut them into 1-inch pieces and place them in a large serving bowl. Drizzle them with dressing, add the olives, and toss gently. Shave a few Parmesan shards over the salad with a vegetable peeler, and serve. This salad keeps in an airtight container in the refrigerator for up to 4 days, unless you stored the veggies for 2 days before dressing them, in which case it will keep for 2 more days.

Roasted Asparagus with Walnuts & Goat Cheese

SERVES 4 TO 6

Roasted asparagus is one of the easiest things to make, and it's so delicious and elegant looking. In the spring, when asparagus is first in season, I like pairing it with chicken, egg dishes, or fish. Here, I dress it up with walnuts and goat cheese, and I like how the warmth of the roasted asparagus slightly melts the goat cheese; the creaminess is a nice foil for the toasted nuts.

2 pounds asparagus, woody ends trimmed

¼ cup extra-virgin olive oil

¼ teaspoon salt

⅛ teaspoon freshly ground black pepper

½ cup walnuts, coarsely chopped and toasted (see Note, page 26)

½ cup crumbled goat cheese

1 teaspoon chopped fresh flat-leaf parsley or tarragon

Heat the oven to 400 degrees.

In a shallow roasting pan, toss the asparagus with the olive oil, salt, and pepper. Roast until tender and cooked through, about 20 minutes. Divide the asparagus among 4 or 6 plates and evenly distribute the walnuts, goat cheese, and herbs over the asparagus. Serve immediately.

Roasted Pumpkin with Scallion, Rosemary, & Raisins

SERVES 4

Every year I roast and puree dozens of little pumpkins for pumpkin pie filling. And as I'm working through pounds and pounds of these babies, I try a few pumpkin side dishes too. This is one of my favorites.

3 sugar baby pumpkins (or another variety of small pie pumpkin or butternut squash)
Salt and freshly ground black pepper
2 tablespoons unsalted butter

2 scallions, sliced
1/4 teaspoon fresh or dried rosemary
1/2 cup freshly squeezed orange juice
1/2 cup raisins
1/4 cup chopped fresh flat-leaf parsley

Heat the oven to 400 degrees.

Break the stems off the pumpkins if they have them, then cut the pumpkins in half and scoop out the seeds. (Reserve the seeds for salting and toasting later; see Note below.)

Season the cut and scooped-out sides with salt and pepper. Place the pumpkin halves, cut side down, in a baking dish or rimmed baking sheet and add 1/4 inch of water to the pan. Bake for about 45 minutes, until tender. Let the pumpkins cool for 10 minutes, then scoop out the flesh in large spoonfuls, trying not to break it up too much, and place it in a bowl.

In a sauté pan, melt the butter over medium heat. Add the scallions and cook, stirring, for about 1 minute. Add the rosemary and cook, stirring, for another minute to bring out its fragrance and flavor. Add the orange juice and raisins and bring the mixture to a boil to plump the raisins slightly. Add the cooked pumpkin flesh and gently fold it into the mixture to combine and warm it through. Taste and season with more salt and pepper, if needed, and the parsley, and serve. This dish keeps in an airtight container in the refrigerator for up to 4 days.

Note: To make toasted pumpkin seeds, heat the oven to 400 degrees. Rinse the seeds in a colander and remove any strands of pumpkin. Dry them between paper towels, then spread them on a sheet pan in a single layer. Sprinkle the seeds liberally with salt. Toast them, turning occasionally to toast evenly, until they are golden brown, about 20 minutes total. Let the seeds cool on the pan, then scrape them off with a spatula.

Fruits

Poached Winter Fruit
with Pomegranate Seeds

Dried Fruit Salad

Pastel Fruit Salad with Green Apples,
Cantaloupe, Honeydew, & Green Grapes

Tropical Fruit Salad

Strawberry Salad with Tarragon &
Blood Orange Juice

Summer Berries in Hibiscus Syrup

Late Summer Fruit Salad

Poached Winter Fruit
with Pomegranate Seeds

SERVES 4

Although I miss the berries and stone fruits of summer during the cold winter months, winter is a fun time to play with creative preparations of citrus fruits, quinces, and pomegranates. This recipe features some of my favorite fruits poached in apple cider (which feels perfect for the season). The harder fruits get more time in the poaching liquid; the softest fruits aren't poached at all, but are soaked in the liquid to pick up some of its flavor.

6 cups apple cider or apple juice

1 cup sugar

2 cinnamon sticks

One 1-inch-wide, 3-inch-long strip
    orange peel

2 quinces, peeled, halved, and cored

2 pears, peeled, halved, and cored

¼ pineapple, peeled, cored, and cut into
    1-inch chunks

2 clementines, peeled and sectioned,
    strings removed

1 banana, sliced crosswise

1 cup pomegranate arils (seeds)

In a medium pot, combine the apple cider, sugar, cinnamon, and orange peel and bring just to a boil over medium-high heat.

Cut the quinces into large pieces and place them in the pot of poaching liquid. Cover and reduce the heat to medium-low to keep the poaching liquid at a gentle simmer. Simmer for 1 hour and 45 minutes. The quinces should turn a light shade of pink.

After 1 hour and 45 minutes, cut the pears into large 1½-inch chunks and place them in the poaching liquid with the quinces. Cook until tender, about 15 minutes more. Add the pineapple pieces and cook for 2 minutes more. Turn off the heat and let cool to room temperature, then add the clementines, bananas, and pomegranate seeds. Chill until ready to serve. To serve, spoon the poached fruit into bowls or cups with some of the poaching liquid. The fruit keeps in an airtight container in the refrigerator for up to 5 days.

Dried Fruit Salad

SERVES 4 TO 6

This fruit salad is good on its own or swirled into yogurt, combined with cottage cheese, or topped off with vanilla ice cream. The easiest way to cut sticky dried fruit is not with a knife, but with scissors. I cook the cherries for less time so they retain more of their intense color. Don't worry about scraping the vanilla bean; I never do it, so I can avoid those little strings that can come with scraping. Just split the bean and throw it in the liquid. It will release the perfect amount of flavor and vanilla "caviar," as I call the seeds.

1 cup sugar

½ cup honey (local, if possible)

¼ cup freshly squeezed lemon juice

½ vanilla bean, split

½ cup dried apricots, cut into strips

½ cup dried pears, cut into ½-inch pieces

½ cup prunes, cut into ½-inch pieces

½ cup dried cherries

1 Honey Crisp apple, cored and cubed

1 star fruit, cut in half and then into ¼-inch-thick slices

1 cup seedless green grapes, halved

In a medium saucepan, combine the sugar, honey, lemon juice, and vanilla bean with 3 cups water. Bring the water to a boil over high heat, then reduce the heat to medium and add the apricots, pears, and prunes. Simmer for 8 minutes, then add the cherries and simmer for 2 minutes more. Turn off the heat and let the fruit sit in the liquid to plump and cool.

Place the apple, star fruit, and grapes in a bowl and pour the slightly cooled cooking liquid and fruits over them. Gently fold to combine and coat. Chill for 30 minutes before serving. Just before serving, drain the cooking liquid and reserve it in an airtight container in the refrigerator; use it later to flavor iced tea or mix it with Prosecco for a cocktail. The salad keeps in an airtight container in the refrigerator for 3 days.

Pastel Fruit Salad with Green Apples, Cantaloupe, Honeydew, & Green Grapes

SERVES 6 TO 8

When I make a fruit salad, I love to feature a color scheme: all reds; red, white, and blue; the colors of the sunset. This one showcases pastel fruits, and it's lovely for a spring meal. The idea for this color scheme came from my favorite Chicago caterers, Hearty Boys. They also have a restaurant and cookbooks, and are among the best at what they do—and they are some of my best friends too.

2 green apples, cut into ³/₄-inch cubes

¹/₂ cantaloupe, peeled, seeded, and cut into ³/₄-inch cubes

¹/₄ honeydew melon, peeled, seeded, and cut into ³/₄-inch cubes

1 cup green grapes, halved

¹/₂ pineapple, peeled, cored, and cut into ³/₄-inch chunks

1 cup pineapple juice

2 tablespoons freshly squeezed lemon juice

4 fresh mint leaves, torn into ¹/₂-inch pieces

Place the apples, cantaloupe, honeydew, grapes, and pineapple in a medium bowl. Pour the pineapple juice and lemon juice over the fruit, add the torn mint, and toss to combine. The flavor of this salad is best if you chill it for at least 30 minutes before serving. The salad keeps in an airtight container in the refrigerator for up to 3 days, but it's best served within 24 hours.

Tropical Fruit Salad

SERVES 4 TO 6

When I was in Bangkok cooking for the World Gourmet Festival, I sampled the most wonderful variety of exotic fruits I've ever tasted in my life, and I love the idea of using some of them at home in this salad. I use local honey whenever I can because studies suggest it helps build up immunity to local ailments!

1 mango, peeled, pitted, and cubed

1 papaya, peeled, seeded, and cubed

1 star fruit, sliced

½ jicama, peeled and cubed

One 15-ounce can lychees, drained and halved

½ pineapple, peeled, cored, and cubed

1 banana, cut crosswise into thick slices

Grated zest of 1 lime

Freshly squeezed juice of 1 lime

1 tablespoon honey (preferably local)

In a mixing bowl, combine the mango, papaya, star fruit, jicama, lychees, pineapple, banana, lime zest, lime juice, and honey and fold gently to coat all the fruit with the citrus juice. Chill, covered, for at least 2 hours before serving. The salad keeps, covered, in the refrigerator for up to 3 days, but it's best served within 24 hours.

Strawberry Salad with Tarragon & Blood Orange Juice

SERVES 4

I love the combination of strawberries and tarragon, an herb with a hint of anise flavor. It's a savory herb, but it's lighter than you might think, and it provides an excellent backdrop for the distinctive fruit flavor of the strawberries. If you can't find blood oranges, try a blushing cara cara orange or another orange with great flavor—look for heirloom oranges, which I've seen at Trader Joe's.

2 blood oranges

1 pint strawberries, roll-cut (see Note)

½ teaspoon snipped fresh tarragon

1 drop pure vanilla extract

Grate the zest of one of the blood oranges into a bowl, then squeeze all the juice from the orange into the bowl with the zest. Peel the other blood orange and use a sharp knife to cut the fruit segments away from the membranes (these membrane-free segments are called suprêmes). Place the suprêmes in the bowl with the blood orange zest and juice and add the strawberries, tarragon, and vanilla. Gently fold everything together with a rubber spatula. Cover and chill for at least 1 hour before serving. The salad keeps in an airtight container in the refrigerator for up to 2 days.

Note: A roll cut, or Japanese roll cut, is a great way to cut strawberries into bite-size pieces that won't stick together the way slices can. Cut the first slice with your knife at a slight angle—with the knife tip at 11 o'clock and the handle at 5 o'clock. Keep the knife at the same angle and roll the strawberry, or whatever you're cutting, a quarter turn, then slice again. Continue until the strawberry is completely sliced into angular chunks.

Summer Berries in Hibiscus Syrup

SERVES 4 TO 6

While working in France for a month during the summer of 2011, I learned a version of this recipe from Chef Daniel Chambon and his son Stephane at the Michelin-starred restaurant (and hotel) Le Pont de l'Ouysse. The restaurant is located in the rocky hills of Dordogne in the heart of truffle and foie gras country, and we rented an old farmhouse nearby. I walked to work every day and my husband and the kids toured the area, one town at a time. We got together in the afternoons between lunch and dinner service for a swim. I felt very lucky to be a chef that summer! These berries are delicious with yogurt.

FOR THE HIBISCUS SYRUP
1 cup sugar
½ cup loose hibiscus tea, or 4 hibiscus
    tea bags

FOR THE BERRIES
½ pint strawberries
½ pint raspberries
½ pint blueberries

In a small saucepan, combine the sugar and 2 cups water and bring the water to a boil over high heat. Turn off the heat and add the hibiscus tea. Let steep for 4 minutes. Strain the hibiscus syrup into a bowl and let cool until lukewarm. Discard the tea leaves. Cut the green tops off the strawberries and then cut them into bite-size chunks. Add the strawberries, raspberries, and blueberries to the hibiscus syrup and let them macerate for at least 1 hour before serving. The berries will keep in an airtight container in the refrigerator for up to 3 days.

Late Summer Fruit Salad

SERVES 4

As a pastry chef, my favorite time of the year is late summer. That's when stone fruits are in season in the Midwest, where I live. I love how fragrant and heady they can be, especially the white peaches. When buying white peaches, check the fragrance of the peach; it should have a floral quality. If you smell that in a white peach when it isn't even ripe yet, you know it will ripen into a gem of a specimen. Another reason I adore late summer? The tomatoes. Sweet, flavorful, eye-blinkingly good tomatoes. Why use them in a fruit salad? Why not! The acid in the tomatoes helps brighten the flavors of the stone fruits. (And tomatoes are fruits too, you know!) As I've mentioned before, try to use local honey to help boost your immune system, deliciously.

1 ripe peach (preferably freestone, which has an easier-to-remove pit)
1 ripe white peach
2 ripe plums
2 ripe apricots

6 cherry tomatoes, halved
6 yellow grape tomatoes, halved
Freshly squeezed juice of 1 lime
2 tablespoons honey (preferably local)

Cut the stone fruits completely around the seam and then twist the halves to "unscrew" one half from the pit. Then cut one more time down the middle of the piece remaining attached to the pit and peel off the sections. Discard the pits. Cut the peaches, plums, and apricots into bite-size pieces and place them in a bowl. Add the tomatoes, lime juice, and honey, then gently fold all the ingredients together to combine. Cover and chill for at least 1 hour before serving (but ideally make this the day before you plan to serve it and chill overnight). The salad keeps in an airtight container in the refrigerator for up to 2 days.

Desserts

Big Chewy Chocolate Chip Cookies

Coconut Pecan Crunch Cookies

Everything Cookies

Cranberry Almond Coconut Bars

Salted Caramel Brownies

Coconut Blueberry Tapioca

Peppermint Meringue Kisses

Madeleines

Homemade Devil Dogs

Chocolate Pudding in a Jar

Blackberry Rice Pudding

Blueberry Ginger Hand Pies

Apple Pie Pops

Myrna's Pie Crust

Lily's Marble Cake

Tangerine Ginger Angel Food Cake

Big Chewy Chocolate Chip Cookies

MAKES 15 TO 20 COOKIES

When I was the answer lady for a chocolate chip–maker's website, the question people asked me most often was, "How can I make my chocolate chip cookies less flat and more puffy?" I get so many requests for big, puffy chocolate chip cookies. So here's my favorite recipe for just that. It has the perfect ratio of flour to butter and sugar for that delicious consistency. Feel free to shake things up with mix-ins like nuts, toffee chips, or dried cherries.

2 cups all-purpose flour

1/2 teaspoon baking soda

1/2 teaspoon salt

3/4 cup (1 1/2 sticks) unsalted butter, melted and cooled

1 cup light brown sugar

1/2 cup sugar

1 teaspoon pure vanilla extract

1 large egg

1 large egg yolk

2 cups bittersweet or semisweet chocolate chips

Position the oven rack in the top third of the oven. Heat the oven to 350 degrees.

In a medium bowl, combine the flour, baking soda, and salt and stir to mix well.

In the bowl of a stand mixer fitted with the paddle attachment, cream together the butter, brown sugar, and sugar on medium speed until very well blended, about 3 minutes. Add the vanilla, egg, and egg yolk and continue mixing until well blended, 1 to 2 minutes.

Add the flour mixture to the butter mixture and mix on low speed just to combine. Add the chips and mix just enough to blend them in. Form golf ball–size balls of dough with your hands. (At this point, you can place the balls on a parchment paper–lined baking sheet, wrap it well with plastic wrap, and freeze. Once frozen, transfer the dough balls to a resealable bag and store in the freezer for up to 1 month, baking them as you need them; thaw the dough balls on a baking sheet for about 30 minutes before baking. But you don't *have* to freeze or chill them.) Space the balls at least 2 inches apart on a baking sheet and bake for 20 to 25 minutes, until golden brown and puffed. Let the cookies cool on the pan. The cookies keep in an airtight container at room temperature for up to 2 weeks.

Coconut Pecan Crunch Cookies

MAKES ABOUT 5 DOZEN COOKIES

I love cookies with unexpected add-ins like potato chips or cornflakes. They give a crunchy texture that reminds me of the almond cookies my mom would grab as an impulse item when she picked up our weekly order of Chinese takeout from Don the Cantonese Chef in Deerfield, Illinois. These cookies have crunch like that, and the great flavor of pecans and coconuts.

1 cup (2 sticks) unsalted butter

1 cup sugar

1½ cups all-purpose flour

1 teaspoon cream of tartar

1 teaspoon baking soda

¼ teaspoon salt

2 cups cornflakes

½ cup chopped pecans, toasted (see Note, page 26)

½ cup sweetened shredded coconut

Position the oven rack in the top third of the oven. Heat the oven to 350 degrees.

In the bowl of a stand mixer fitted with the paddle attachment, cream the butter and sugar until well combined and slightly fluffy, about 5 minutes. Add the flour, cream of tartar, baking soda, and salt, and mix well. Add the cornflakes, pecans, and coconut and mix on low speed until just incorporated. Cover and chill the dough for 1 hour.

Using an ice cream scoop, scoop 1½-inch balls of dough onto ungreased baking sheets, spacing them 2 inches apart to allow for spreading. (At this point, you can place the balls on a parchment paper–lined baking sheet, wrap it well with plastic wrap, and freeze. Once frozen, transfer the dough balls to a resealable bag and store in the freezer for up to 1 month, baking them as you need them; thaw the dough balls on a baking sheet for about 30 minutes before baking.)

Bake for 10 to 12 minutes, until very lightly browned. Let the cookies cool on the baking sheet for 2 minutes before transferring them to a wire rack to cool completely. The cookies keep in an airtight container at room temperature for up to 5 days.

Everything Cookies

MAKES ABOUT 6 DOZEN SMALL COOKIES

This is the "everything bagel" of cookies. It contains practically every mix-in you could think of: coconut, toffee bits, oatmeal, almonds, and raisins. It has a great crunchy exterior with a chewy inside chock-full of texture and flavor.

1 cup (2 sticks) unsalted butter, cut into pieces to warm up slightly

1 cup sugar

1 cup light brown sugar

1 teaspoon pure vanilla extract

2 large eggs

2 cups all-purpose flour

½ teaspoon salt

¼ teaspoon baking soda

One 8-ounce bag toffee candy bits

1 cup old-fashioned oats (not quick-cooking)

1 cup sweetened flake coconut

1 cup slivered almonds (with skin)

1 cup raisins

Position the oven rack in the top third of the oven. Heat the oven to 350 degrees.

In the bowl of a stand mixer fitted with the paddle attachment, cream the butter, sugar, brown sugar, and vanilla on medium-low speed for about 5 minutes. Add the eggs and mix until well combined, about 3 minutes. In a separate bowl, stir the flour, salt, and baking soda together, then add it slowly to the wet ingredients and mix thoroughly on low speed for 2 to 3 minutes. Add the toffee bits, oats, coconut, almonds, and raisins and mix until just incorporated. Drop the cookie dough by teaspoons, spaced 2 inches apart, onto an ungreased baking sheet. (At this point, you can place the balls on a parchment paper–lined baking sheet, wrap it well with plastic wrap, and freeze. Once frozen, transfer the dough balls to a resealable bag and store in the freezer for up to 1 month, baking them as you need them; thaw the dough balls on a baking sheet for about 30 minutes before baking.) Bake for 15 to 18 minutes. Let the cookies cool on the pan. The cookies keep in an airtight container at room temperature for up to 1 week.

Cranberry Almond Coconut Bars

MAKES 12 BARS

Bar cookies travel well and provide a sweet energy boost when you need one. This bar has it all: buttery crust, tart and chewy filling, and chocolate on top. (And I love how easy the chocolate topping is!)

FOR THE CRUST

6 tablespoons cold unsalted butter, cut into ½-inch pieces

½ cup packed light brown sugar

½ teaspoon salt

1 cup all-purpose flour

½ cup finely chopped almonds

FOR THE FILLING

2 large eggs

1 tablespoon milk

2 teaspoons pure vanilla extract

1 tablespoon grated orange zest

1 cup sugar

2 tablespoons all-purpose flour

½ teaspoon baking powder

¼ teaspoon salt

1 cup coarsely chopped fresh cranberries (a food processor works nicely for chopping cranberries)

½ cup sweetened flake coconut

½ cup coarsely chopped almonds

FOR THE TOPPING

1 cup best-quality semisweet chocolate chips (for melting)

Heat the oven to 350 degrees.

Make the crust: In the bowl of a stand mixer fitted with the paddle attachment, cream the butter, brown sugar, and salt on low speed for 3 to 5 minutes. Add the flour and almonds and mix on low speed until well combined. Press the mixture into the bottom of an ungreased 9-inch square baking pan. Bake for 15 to 20 minutes, until golden brown all over.

Make the filling: While the crust is baking, whisk the eggs in a medium bowl, then whisk in the milk, vanilla, and orange zest. Use a wooden spoon to stir in the sugar, flour, baking powder, and salt, then stir in the cranberries, coconut, and almonds.

Spread the filling evenly over the baked crust and return the baking pan to the oven to bake for 30 minutes more.

Take the bars out of the oven and immediately sprinkle the chocolate chips over the uncut surface. Let the heat from the bars melt the chocolate to make a chocolate layer, spreading the chocolate with a spatula if needed to cover the surface completely. Let the bars cool completely in the pan, set on a wire rack. The chocolate will set up as it cools. Cut into individual bars for serving. The bars keep in an airtight container at room temperature for up to 1 week.

Salted Caramel Brownies

MAKES ABOUT 12 BROWNIES

As you might expect, I've made countless brownies and tried a lot of different brownie recipes. This has truly become my favorite. It features just a handful of ingredients, with chunks of chewy caramel and extra salt. (Also, it only requires one bowl, which makes my dishwasher—ahem, my husband—happy.) The key with such a simple recipe is using good ingredients. If you can find Callebaut unsweetened chocolate, use it, and your brownies will taste just like mine.

4 ounces good-quality unsweetened chocolate, chopped

¾ cup (1½ sticks) unsalted butter

1½ cups sugar

3 large eggs

1 teaspoon pure vanilla extract

1 cup all-purpose flour

½ teaspoon kosher or sea salt plus ¼ more for sprinkling

1 cup (7 ounces) chopped chewy caramels, such as Werther's (I use scissors to chop them)

Heat the oven to 350 degrees. Line an 8-inch square baking pan with parchment paper.

In a large microwave-proof bowl, melt the chocolate and butter together in the microwave. Start with 1 minute, and then heat in 30-second intervals, stirring between intervals, until the chocolate and butter are completely melted. Use a wooden spoon to stir the sugar into the melted chocolate mixture, then stir in the eggs and vanilla extract. Stir in the flour and ½ teaspoon salt until thoroughly combined, then stir in the caramels. Pour the batter into the prepared pan, smooth the top, and sprinkle the remaining ¼ teaspoon salt over the surface. Bake for 25 to 30 minutes, until the brownies are set on top and start to puff up a bit. Let the brownies cool completely in the pan, and then cut them into bars. If you want very clean cuts, cover and chill the brownies for a few hours or let sit at room temperature overnight, and then cut them while they are cold. (Let them come back to room temperature before serving, or you can put them in a lunch box while still cold.) The brownies keep, covered, at room temperature for up to 5 days or in the refrigerator for up to 2 weeks.

Coconut Blueberry Tapioca

SERVES 4

I can't decide if this is a really old-fashioned dessert or a really current trendy dessert. I did something like it when I was pastry chef at Tru, the fancy-pants fine dining restaurant I opened in Chicago in 1999, but it had a few more moving parts, like meringue kisses, tiny pineapple cubes, a passion fruit drizzle, and some other elements I can't even remember. What I do remember is that it was delicious. Adding the blueberries at the end helps give a burst of juiciness when you eat a spoonful.

½ cup small- or large-grain tapioca
2 cups milk
½ cup coconut milk

6 tablespoons sugar
½ teaspoon pure vanilla extract
1 cup blueberries

Soak the tapioca in water overnight in a covered container in the refrigerator, if you have the time. Drain the next day. Place the tapioca, milk, coconut milk, sugar, and 1 cup water in a large saucepan over medium-low heat and simmer, stirring occasionally, for 20 minutes, until the tapioca is tender. (If you haven't soaked the tapioca, it may take an additional 10 minutes of simmering to get to the right tenderness.) Turn off the heat and stir in the vanilla extract, then stir in the blueberries. Place the tapioca in an airtight container (you can portion it into smaller containers at this point if you'd like, for easy transport) and refrigerate for at least 2 hours before serving, or up to 3 days. It will thicken as it chills.

Peppermint Meringue Kisses

MAKES 50 TO 75 PIECES

These are light, minty, end-of-lunch nibbles. They are also great as a garnish for Chocolate Pudding in a Jar (page 220). The marbleized red coloring is so pretty and especially appropriate during the winter holidays. I like to package them in clear cellophane bags, twelve to a bag, tie them with a colorful ribbon, and give them as a hostess gift.

½ cup egg whites (from about 3 eggs)

1 pinch salt

1 pinch cream of tartar

⅓ cup sugar

½ cup confectioners' sugar

⅛ teaspoon mint extract

6 drops red food coloring

Heat the oven to 200 degrees and line 2 or 3 baking sheets with parchment paper.

In the bowl of a stand mixer fitted with the whisk attachment, whisk the egg whites with the salt and cream of tartar on medium speed until soft peaks form, about 3 minutes. Add the sugar in 3 batches, whipping on medium-high speed for 1 minute between additions, then add the confectioners' sugar and whip for 30 seconds on low speed. Add the mint extract and mix for 30 seconds more. Remove the bowl from the mixer and dot the surface with the red food coloring. Using a rubber spatula, swirl through the whites just one time to marble the color slightly, then load it into a pastry bag fitted with a large plain tip. (The color will swirl as you pipe the meringue out of the bag.) Pipe kisses about 1¼ inches in diameter onto the parchment-lined baking sheets and bake for 2 hours, checking after an hour to make sure they aren't browning at all (if they are, turn the oven down to 175 degrees). After 2 hours, turn the oven off, but keep the door closed, and let the kisses cool in the oven for another hour, or up to 12 hours. Peel off of the parchment paper to serve. The kisses keep in an airtight container at room temperature for up to 5 days.

Madeleines

MAKES 24

These little lemony shell-shaped French sponge cakes are a nice, simple way to finish lunch. I love having one with a cup of tea or coffee to dunk it in. My madeleine pans, or plaques, *as they are called in France, have twelve shell-shaped depressions in them. I have two of them—and they once belonged to Julia Child. I know I'm lucky to be the caretaker of such a treasure. People tend to give me their family heirloom baking equipment because they know I love it, use it, and I'll take good care of it.*

10 tablespoons (1¼ sticks) unsalted butter, melted, plus softened butter for the pans

1 scant cup all-purpose flour, plus more for dusting the pans

3 large eggs

⅔ cup sugar

1 teaspoon pure vanilla extract

½ teaspoon grated lemon zest

¾ teaspoon baking powder

¼ teaspoon salt

Confectioners' sugar, for dusting

Heat the oven to 375 degrees. Using softened butter and a pastry brush, generously butter 2 madeleine pans, then dust them lightly with flour and knock out any excess.

In the bowl of a stand mixer fitted with the whisk attachment, whip the eggs with the sugar until light and fluffy, then whisk in the vanilla and lemon zest.

In a separate bowl, stir together the flour, baking powder, and salt. With the mixer on low speed, slowly add the flour mixture to the egg mixture, then slowly drizzle in the melted butter. Transfer the batter to a piping bag with a large plain tip. Refrigerate if desired, for up to 3 days, to hold the batter for later and make it easier to pipe.

Pipe batter into each depression of the madeleine pan until almost full. Don't worry about smoothing the top; the batter will smooth out on its own as it bakes.

Bake for 10 to 14 minutes, until light golden brown. There should be a bump on the top of each madeleine, which will later become the bottom of the cake. Remove the pan from the oven and immediately whack it on the counter to knock the madeleines out of the pan. Place the madeleines on a platter and sprinkle them with confectioners' sugar before serving. The madeleines are best eaten within 24 hours. Store them in an airtight bag at room temperature.

Chocolate Pudding in a Jar

SERVES 4

This is the simplest chocolate pudding and also one of the richest and best tasting. It's so smooth, and intensely chocolaty, even though it doesn't call for much chocolate. When you use quality chocolate—which you definitely should do here—a little goes a long way. It's also gluten-free. Placing it in a jar makes it easy to transport, and looks very cute (see opposite). If you're taking these jars on a picnic, bring a can of whipped cream packed with an ice pack, and top each serving with a rosette of whipped cream.

2 cups heavy cream

1 pinch salt

2 ounces bittersweet chocolate, chopped

3 large egg yolks

¼ cup sugar

In a saucepan, combine the cream and salt and bring to a boil over medium-high heat. As soon as the cream boils, remove the pan from the heat and add the chopped chocolate, whisking until the chocolate melts. Put the saucepan back on the stove with the heat off.

In a medium bowl, whisk the egg yolks and sugar together. A little at a time, add the hot chocolate mixture to the egg mixture, whisking constantly. (Be sure not to add too much of the hot mixture to the eggs at once, or you'll curdle the egg yolks.)

Pour the pudding mixture back into the saucepan and heat it over medium heat, whisking slowly, until it thickens slightly and you see a few boiling bubbles in the center of the pot, 3 to 5 minutes. The mixture should be thick enough to coat the back of a wooden spoon. Run your finger down the back of the spoon; when the edges do not blur, the mixture is ready.

Divide the pudding among four 6- or 8-ounce canning jars. Tightly cover each jar with plastic wrap or a lid. Refrigerate for at least 4 hours, or until ready to serve. The pudding keeps in the jars in the refrigerator for up to 5 days.

RIGHT: *Chocolate Pudding in a Jar and Homemade Devil Dogs (page 222)*

Homemade Devil Dogs

MAKES 15 TO 18

I love the idea of regional food, and I think of Devil Dogs as just that, from the East Coast. My husband grew up in East Islip, New York, on Long Island, and always raved about eating these chocolate sandwich cakes with creamy filling. When I went searching for the perfect dessert for his birthday one year, I thought I'd buy Devil Dogs to serve, but to my frustration they weren't sold in the Midwest. So of course I thought, "I'll make them!" My dear friend Ina Pinkney, who is from Brooklyn, shared her recipe with me. Thank you, Ina!

FOR THE CAKE
2 cups all-purpose flour
1 cup sugar
½ cup cocoa powder
1 teaspoon baking soda
½ teaspoon salt

6 tablespoons unsalted butter, melted
¾ cup milk
1 large egg
1 teaspoon pure vanilla extract

1 recipe Marshmallow Cream (page 223)

In the bowl of a stand mixer fitted with the whisk attachment, combine the flour, sugar, cocoa powder, baking soda, and salt. Whisk for 30 seconds on low speed. Add the melted butter, milk, egg, and vanilla and mix on low speed for 1 minute to combine, then raise the speed to medium and mix for 2 minutes to make a smooth batter.

Heat oven to 350 degrees. Line 2 baking sheets with parchment paper.

Transfer the batter to a pastry bag fitted with a large plain tip. Pipe 30 to 36 bone-shaped fingers, 3 inches long and 1 inch wide (kind of like the shape of a Milano cookie but a bit wider at the ends), in rows 1½ inches apart on each baking sheet.

Bake for 9 to 10 minutes, until the cakes are puffy and firm to the touch. Remove from the oven and let cool completely on the baking sheets.

Peel the cooled cakes off the parchment paper and lay them flat side up on a baking sheet. Pipe marshmallow cream over the surface to cover, chill for 10 minutes to allow the cream to stiffen, then place a second cake on top to make a sandwich. Repeat with the remaining cakes and filling. Cover and chill for at least 1 hour before serving. The devil dogs keep, covered, in the refrigerator for up to 5 days, or you can freeze the assembled cakes in an airtight container for up to 2 months.

Marshmallow Cream

MAKES ENOUGH TO FILL 15 TO 18 DEVIL DOGS

6 tablespoons unsalted
  butter, softened

1 cup confectioners'
  sugar

One 7-ounce jar
  marshmallow cream
  (1½ cups)

1 teaspoon pure vanilla
  extract

Place the butter in the bowl of a stand mixer fitted with the whisk attachment and cream until fluffy, about 4 minutes. Add the confectioners' sugar, marshmallow cream, and vanilla and continue mixing on low speed until combined, smooth, and fluffy, about 2 minutes. Transfer the cream to a pastry bag with the same large plain tip that you used for the cake batter (clean it before piping the filling) and pipe it onto the cakes as directed.

Blackberry Rice Pudding

SERVES 4 TO 6

When I lived in England for three years, I developed a love for British-style rice pudding. It's loose and creamy, unlike the baked American version, which is often so firm it could be cut into blocks. It starts with what they call "pudding rice," a starchy short-grained rice reserved for rice pudding. The closest approximations are Arborio rice, which is usually used for risotto, and Japanese sticky rice, usually the go-to rice for making sushi. Either of these works well in rice pudding. I love that this dessert is all prepared on the stovetop— no oven to preheat!

1 cup short-grain rice (such as Arborio or Japanese sticky rice), rinsed in a colander until the water runs clear

4½ cups milk

¼ vanilla bean, split lengthwise

½ teaspoon grated lemon zest

4 large egg yolks

½ cup sugar

2 cups halved fresh blackberries

In a heavy saucepan, combine the rice, milk, vanilla bean, and lemon zest and bring to a simmer over medium heat. Immediately reduce the heat to as low as possible, cover tightly, and simmer gently, stirring occasionally, until the rice is very tender, 20 to 25 minutes. Turn off the heat.

Stir the egg yolks into the cooked rice mixture and cook on low just until thickened, 1 to 2 minutes. Stir in the sugar to dissolve it, then gently stir in the blackberries.

Pour the rice pudding into ramekins or dessert cups and serve immediately or cover tightly with plastic wrap and refrigerate until ready to serve. The rice pudding keeps in an airtight container in the refrigerator for up to 4 days.

Blueberry Ginger Hand Pies

MAKES 7 TO 10 HAND PIES

July means blueberry picking for my family and me. We always seem to pick way more than we can eat. We freeze some for the dark days of winter and weekend blueberry pancake production, and we also love using them in these delicious handheld pies. I've been seeing hand pies more and more often lately, and pastry chefs love making them because you can get creative and fill them with just about anything!

FOR THE PIES

1 cup fresh or frozen blueberries

½ cup blueberry preserves

1 tablespoon cornstarch

Grated zest of ½ lemon

1 tablespoon chopped crystallized ginger

½ recipe Myrna's Pie Crust (page 230), or store-bought pie dough for 1 crust

FOR THE GLAZE

½ cup confectioners' sugar

Grated zest of ½ lemon

Freshly squeezed juice of ½ lemon

Heat the oven to 425 degrees. Line a baking sheet with parchment paper.

In a medium bowl, combine the blueberries, preserves, cornstarch, lemon zest, and ginger.

Roll the dough out to ⅛ inch thick. Using a biscuit cutter, cut 4½-inch round discs of pie dough. Lay the discs on the lined baking sheet. Use a pastry brush to brush water around the edge of a disc, and place a heaping tablespoon of filling in the center. Fold the dough over the filling to make a half-moon shape and carefully seal the pie's edge with your fingers, then crimp it with a fork. Repeat with the remaining dough discs and filling. Chill the hand pies for 15 minutes to help the edges really stick together. Bake for 15 to 20 minutes, until golden brown. Let the pies cool for 20 minutes on the baking sheet.

Stir together the confectioners' sugar, lemon zest, and lemon juice to make a glaze. Brush the pies with the lemon glaze and let them cool for an additional 20 minutes. Serve warm or room temperature. The hand pies are best served the day you make them, but they keep in an airtight container at room temperature for up to 3 days.

Apple Pie Pops

MAKES 8 POPS

These cute desserts contain all the ingredients of an apple pie, but on a stick. That makes them easy to transport and pack and just plain fun to eat. The sprinkling of cinnamon sugar on the outside is partly for flavor and partly for a touch of sparkle.

1 recipe Myrna's Pie Crust (page 230), or store-bought double-crust pie dough

8 ice-pop sticks

8 teaspoons apple butter (page 57) or store bought

Four ¾-inch-square chewy caramels, halved

32 raisins

¼ teaspoon ground cinnamon

¼ cup sugar

Heat the oven to 425 degrees. Line a baking sheet with parchment paper

Roll the pie dough out to ⅛ inch thick. Using a 2½-inch biscuit cutter, cut out sixteen 2½-inch circles of pie dough. Lay 8 of the circles on the lined baking sheet. Brush water around the edges of those circles and position the ice-pop sticks on the circles so about 1 inch of the stick extends into the center of the circle.

Place 1 teaspoon of apple butter in the center of each circle. Place 1 piece of caramel and 4 raisins on top of the apple butter. Place a second circle of pie dough on top and carefully seal the pies with your fingers, being careful to keep the filling inside, then crimp the edge with a fork.

Combine the cinnamon with the sugar. Brush the surface of each pie with water and sprinkle with cinnamon sugar. Bake for 15 to 20 minutes, until golden brown. Let the pies cool completely on the baking sheet. To keep the pops intact, pick them up off the pan by the pie crust, not the stick. The pie pops keep in an airtight container at room temperature for up to 3 days.

Myrna's Pie Crust

MAKES TWO 9-INCH PIE CRUSTS

My mom, Myrna, was a stellar baker and pie maker. Her secret for making excellent pie crust was adding a little vinegar to the dough. The acid in the vinegar inhibits the development of gluten, and the result is a crust that's flaky and tender, not tough. Her other secret was that she had bad circulation—giving her perpetually cold hands. I have that too, and it certainly is helpful when you're working with pie dough. If your hands run warm, try dipping them in ice water before handling the dough.

8 tablespoons (1 stick) unsalted butter, chilled

½ cup shortening

1 ice cube

2 teaspoons red wine vinegar

3 cups all-purpose flour

1 teaspoon salt

1 teaspoon sugar

Cut the chilled butter into small cubes and refrigerate it again while you prepare the shortening. Use a rubber spatula to spread the shortening about ¼ inch thick on a piece of foil (it will be about a 6-inch square). Score the shortening with the edge of the spatula to make a grid of ½-inch squares, and then freeze it for 20 minutes. This will make cubes of shortening.

Place an ice cube in a 1-cup measuring cup, add enough water to bring it up to the ½-cup mark, then add the vinegar. Set the cup aside until the ice cube is just melted and the water and vinegar are cold.

In the bowl of a stand mixer fitted with the paddle attachment, combine the flour, salt, sugar, chilled butter, and frozen shortening (bend the foil back to release the shortening from the foil) and mix on low speed until the butter and shortening pieces are the size of large peas. Add the ice water–vinegar mixture and raise the mixer speed to medium-low. (You might need another teaspoon or so of water to bring the dough together.) Count to 25, then turn off the mixer. Shape the dough into 2 discs, wrap them in plastic wrap, and refrigerate for at least 2 hours or overnight. The dough keeps for up to 3 days in the refrigerator and 2 months in the freezer.

Lily's Marble Cake

SERVES 12

I'm sharing this delicious recipe in honor of Florence Shay and Lily Gerson. As a kid I cut through the yards in my neighborhood to go to my friend Lauren Shay's house. When Lauren's grandma Lily visited, she always made an irresistible chocolate marble cake. I tried to get the recipe from Lauren's mom, Florence, but she wouldn't share it. Then I became a professional pastry chef, and I tried to re-create the recipe. But I never got it right. I contacted the family again, but they still wouldn't give it up. For forty years I tried to get that recipe, badgering Florence's husband, children, and grandchildren for it. Nope! Nothing. Then, finally, Florence shared it with me on my wedding day, as my wedding gift. And what a gift it was.

1 cup (2 sticks) unsalted butter, plus more for the pan

2½ cups all-purpose flour, plus more for the pan

2 cups sugar

4 large eggs

2 teaspoons baking powder

1 pinch salt

1 teaspoon pure vanilla extract

1 cup milk

3 tablespoons cocoa powder

1⅓ cups sweetened shredded coconut

Heat the oven to 350 degrees. Butter and flour a tube pan.

In the bowl of a stand mixer fitted with the paddle attachment, cream the butter until light and fluffy, about 5 minutes. Add the sugar and continue to mix on medium speed for about 1 minute. Add the eggs one at a time, beating for 30 seconds after each addition.

In a separate bowl, use a wooden spoon to stir the baking powder and salt into the flour until thoroughly distributed. In another small bowl, mix the vanilla into the milk. Alternately add the milk mixture (in 3 increments) and the flour mixture (in 2 increments) to the butter mixture, mixing after each addition. Continue mixing for 5 minutes after you've added all the milk and flour (beating for a long time is important here). Divide the batter into thirds, and mix one-third of it with the cocoa powder. Stir the coconut into the remaining golden batter.

Pour the golden batter into the prepared pan, then spoon the chocolate batter around on top. Draw a knife through the batters to swirl the chocolate batter into the golden batter. Do not stir. Bake for about 1 hour and 15 minutes, until a toothpick inserted into the cake comes out clean. Let cool completely in the pan, then turn out the cake, slice, and serve, or wrap in plastic wrap for later. This cake is better the second day and keeps, well wrapped, for up to 1 week at room temperature.

Tangerine Ginger Angel Food Cake

SERVES 8

When I was a child my favorite kind of cake was angel food cake. I always ate it on my birthday, and I still do! I love the light, airy texture, and now I appreciate how low in fat it is. To make the cake look white and, well, angelic, I run a table knife around the wall of the traditional tube pan it's baked in, which detaches the cake from the browned crumbs (they stay behind, stuck to the wall of the pan) and releases a lovely white confection. Using cake flour, which is lower in protein than all-purpose flour, makes the cake tender and feather light. This is delicious with whipped cream and ripe fruit, such as chopped peaches tossed with blackberries.

FOR THE CAKE

1½ cups sugar

2 teaspoons ground ginger

1⅛ cups sifted cake flour

1½ cups egg whites (from about 1 dozen large eggs)

1¼ teaspoons cream of tartar

½ teaspoon salt

1 teaspoon pure vanilla extract

Grated zest of 1 tangerine or orange

FOR THE GLAZE

¼ cup freshly squeezed tangerine juice or orange juice

1 tablespoon egg whites (from about 1 large egg)

2 cups confectioners' sugar

2 tablespoons finely chopped crystallized ginger

Heat the oven to 375 degrees.

Make the cake: Sift ½ cup of the sugar, the ground ginger, and the sifted cake flour into a bowl. Sift 2 more times to aerate the mixture. Set aside.

In the bowl of a stand mixer fitted with the whisk attachment (or using a hand mixer), whip the egg whites until foamy. Add the cream of tartar and salt and continue whipping until soft peaks form. With the mixer running, gradually add the remaining 1 cup sugar and continue whipping until the mixture is stiff and the sugar has dissolved, about 30 seconds.

Using a rubber spatula, fold the flour mixture into the egg whites in 3 increments, then fold in the vanilla and tangerine zest. Spoon the batter into an ungreased tube pan and smooth out the top if needed. Bake until light golden brown, 30 to 35 minutes. Cool by

hanging the cake (in the pan) upside down on the neck of a wine bottle or 12-ounce soda bottle until it cools to room temperature. Remove the cake from the bottle and run a table knife blade around the edge of the cake to loosen it and leave the outer crumbs attached to the pan wall, then knock the cake out onto a plate. The outside of the cake will remain in the pan, leaving the turned-out cake whiter and more angelic.

Make the glaze: Stir the tangerine juice, egg whites, confectioners' sugar, and crystallized ginger together until the sugar is completely incorporated. Pour the glaze over the top of the cake and spread it with a spatula, letting the glaze trickle down the sides. Let set for at least 30 minutes, until the glaze is firm, before serving. Cut the cake with a serrated knife, using a sawing motion. The cake keeps, wrapped well, at room temperature for up to 4 days.

Drinks

Sparkling Strawberry Lime Lemonade

Mango Lemonade

Blueberry Mint Lemonade

Pineapple Limeade

Homemade Ginger Ale

Spritzers

Citron Pressé

Iced Teas & Tisanes

Custom Ice Cubes

Apricot Lime Sparkler

Prosecco with Mango & Strawberries

Lunchtime Wine

Sparkling Strawberry Lime Lemonade

SERVES 6 TO 8

During the hot months I love to make signature cold drinks with lemonade as the starting point. Here's one that's pretty in pink, thanks to strawberries, and extra-refreshing with effervescent lime seltzer and a fresh lime garnish. Add a shot of gin to a glass of this lemonade for a cocktail with a kick.

1 lime, cut into 6 to 8 wedges

Ice

1 cup hulled and chopped strawberries

1 cup sugar

1 cup lemon juice, preferably freshly squeezed

2 cups chilled lime seltzer

Place 1 lime wedge in each of six to eight 10-ounce glasses. Add enough ice to fill the glasses halfway. Combine the strawberries, sugar, lemon juice, and 2 cups water in a blender and blend until the strawberries are pureed. Divide among the glasses. Top off each glass with the seltzer water and serve.

Mango Lemonade

SERVES 6 TO 8

Straight mango is too thick for a refreshing drink, but pair it with lemon juice and water, and sweeten it a bit, and you've got a party in a glass. Add a shot of vodka to make a summer cocktail.

Ice
1 cup ripe mango chunks
1 cup sugar

1 cup lemon juice, preferably freshly squeezed

Fill six to eight 10-ounce glasses halfway with ice. Combine the mango, sugar, lemon juice, and 4 cups water in a blender and blend until the mango is pureed. Divide among the glasses and serve. The lemonade keeps in a covered bottle or pitcher in the refrigerator for up to 1 week.

Blueberry Mint Lemonade

SERVES 6 TO 8

While making blueberry sorbet one day, I tasted the blueberry puree I was about to freeze and thought, "This would make an outstanding drink." It does. And here it is.

6 to 8 fresh mint sprigs
Ice
1 cup blueberries

1 cup sugar
1 cup lemon juice, preferably freshly squeezed

Place 1 sprig of mint in each of six to eight 10-ounce glasses. Add enough ice to fill the glasses halfway. Combine the blueberries, sugar, lemon juice, and 4 cups water in a blender and blend until the blueberries are pureed. Divide among the glasses and serve. The lemonade keeps in a covered bottle or pitcher in the refrigerator for up to 1 week.

Pineapple Limeade

SERVES 6 TO 8

I used to make pineapple water for the staff meal at Tru. I'd make it by boiling pineapple rinds (left over from our signature pineapple carpaccio). This is a tribute to the refreshing pineapple flavor we all enjoyed during those days.

1 lime, cut into wedges

Ice

1 cup pineapple juice

1 cup sugar

1 cup lime juice, preferably freshly squeezed

Place 1 lime wedge in each of six to eight 10-ounce glasses. Add enough ice to fill the glasses halfway. Combine the pineapple juice, sugar, lime juice, and 4 cups water in a pitcher and stir until the sugar is dissolved. Divide among the glasses and serve. The limeade keeps in a covered bottle or pitcher in the refrigerator for up to 1 week.

Homemade Ginger Ale

SERVES 4

I make my own root beer using cinnamon, ginger, and vanilla—in ginormous batches, usually 12,000 bottles at a time. But you can make other soda pops at home in much smaller batches than that. Here's how to make your own homemade ginger ale, which is much more flavorful than store-bought, because it's the real thing.

1 cup sugar

Twelve 1/8-inch slices peeled fresh ginger root

2 drops pure vanilla extract

1 quart seltzer water (or club soda if you prefer a bit less sharpness)

In a saucepan, combine the sugar and ginger slices with 1 cup water and bring to a boil. Turn the heat off, let cool, add the vanilla, and use immediately or refrigerate the ginger simple syrup until ready to use, up to 2 weeks. To serve, place 1/4 cup of strained ginger simple syrup into each of 4 glasses over ice, then top each glass off with 1 cup of the seltzer.

Spritzers

Wine spritzers are simple, summery cocktails that combine wine with sparkling water or soda water. They're lower in calories and alcohol than a glass of wine, which is nice during the day.

Chianti Spritzer

SERVES 1

Ice

½ cup Chianti (or another light, fruity
    red wine)

¼ cup sparkling water or soda water

1 orange slice

Fill a stemmed wine glass halfway with ice. Pour the Chianti over the ice, then add the sparkling water or soda water. Cut a slit into the orange slice, slip it onto the side of the glass, and serve.

Sauvignon Blanc Spritzer

SERVES 1

Ice

½ cup Sauvignon Blanc (or another light,
    fruity white wine)

¼ cup sparkling water or soda water

1 lemon slice

Fill a stemmed wine glass halfway with ice. Pour the Sauvignon Blanc over the ice, then add the sparkling water or soda water. Cut a slit into the lemon slice, slip it onto the side of the glass, and serve.

Citron Pressé

SERVES 1

This is a refreshing (and incredibly simple) drink that I enjoy all over France. It's almost always available in cafés and bistros there. It's especially good when you've maybe eaten a little too much of a good thing too many days in a row. You can adjust the amount of sugar to make it as sweet or tart as you personally like. It's basically a DIY lemonade. Maybe that's why I like it so much.

2 ice cubes

2 tablespoons freshly squeezed lemon
    juice

1 to 2 tablespoons sugar, to taste

Place the ice cubes and lemon juice in a tall 10-ounce glass. Top off the glass with about 1 cup water and serve with the sugar on the side and an iced-tea spoon for stirring. Stir in as much sugar as desired for the sweetness you like.

Iced Teas & Tisanes

Iced tea (along with a few other life-changing foods, including ice cream cones) became popular in the United States after the 1904 World's Fair in St. Louis. But the idea of drinking iced tea is still a bit foreign in one of the biggest tea-drinking countries in the world, England. When I worked and lived there in the early 1990s, my brother came to visit and tried to order an iced tea at a hotel. The server said they didn't have it. My wisecracking brother said, "You got tea?" (The server nodded.) "You got ice?" (The server nodded again.) "Well, put them together, and you got iced tea." And my brother got his iced tea—he always gets his way. While I don't recommend trying that when you visit England, I do love iced tea, and it's a fantastic lunchtime drink. Here's a quick primer on how to make it.

Iced tea, like hot tea, is made with leaves from the tea plant, also known as *Camellia sinensis,* steeped in very hot or boiling water. (All kinds of tea come from the same plant. A tisane, or herbal tea, is made the same way, but with leaves, herbs, or flowers that are not from the tea plant and usually contain no caffeine.) To make iced tea or an iced tisane, you just chill the tea and pour it over ice.

Start with cold water, preferably filtered. Cold water has the most oxygen in it, which provides a cleaner flavor. For black tea and tisanes, bring the water just to a boil (just 212 degrees, before a hard rolling boil kicks in). For green teas, white teas, and lighter oolong teas, heat your water to 180 degrees—hot, but not boiling.

Pour the hot water over the tea or herbs. You can use loose tea (I like to put it in a mesh tea ball) or a tea bag. Use about 1 teaspoon of loose tea per cup of water, or a bit more if you are using loose tea with bigger, fuller leaves or tisanes with larger leaves or blossoms. Steep the tea for 3 to 5 minutes for most black teas and tisanes. For green and white teas, steep for 2 to 3 minutes. Remove the tea either by straining it or removing the bag or tea ball. Let the tea cool for 30 minutes, then chill it for 2 to 3 hours before serving it over ice.

Iced Black Tea

1 teaspoon loose black tea or 1 tea bag   8 ounces cold filtered water

Heat the water just until boiling, then immediately pour it over the tea leaves in a teapot or heatproof container. Let steep for 3 to 5 minutes, then remove the tea leaves and let the tea cool for 30 minutes. Chill, covered, until ready to serve, or up to 5 days. Serve over ice. You may sweeten the tea, if desired, with sugar, raw sugar, stevia, agave, simple syrup, or a flavored simple syrup (recipe follows).

VARIATIONS

- Steep the tea and mix in ⅓ cup fruit juice before serving

- Steep the tea and mix in 1 to 2 tablespoons citrus juice (1 tablespoon for lemon or lime juice, 2 tablespoons for orange or grapefruit) before serving

- Add citrus peel to the tea leaves before steeping (bergamot rind or oil is the citrus flavor used to make Earl Grey tea)

- Add spices (1 cinnamon stick, 4 whole allspice, or 2 cloves per cup of water) to the tea leaves before steeping

- Combine tea leaves and tisanes and brew them together

Vanilla Simple Syrup

This is a sweet addition (literally) to tea. I like to serve unsweetened iced tea with a small pitcher of simple syrup on the side so guests can sweeten their tea to suit their own taste.

1 cup sugar   ½ vanilla bean, split but not scraped

Combine the sugar, vanilla bean, and 2 cups water in a small saucepan and bring to a boil. Turn off the heat and let cool for 10 minutes to infuse the flavor. The simple syrup keeps in an airtight container in the refrigerator for up to 1 month.

Custom
Ice Cubes

You can make signature ice cubes to add additional flavors and visual excitement to your iced teas. Fill the chambers of an ice cube tray with fruit, such as raspberries, or citrus, such as pieces of lemon peel, or edible flowers, such as pansy petals, or herbs, such as mint leaves. Then pour in water, juice, or leftover tea to fill the chambers and freeze. (If you use tea, the cubes will add flavor and not water down a glass of iced tea as they thaw.) And look for some of the great ice cube trays available in specialty cookware stores—big blocky cubes good for retro cocktails, long thin strips that can slide into water bottles, and even Lego and heart-shaped ones!

Raspberry Lemon Ice Cubes

24 small strips lemon zest   24 raspberries

Using a 12-cube ice cube tray, place 2 raspberries and 2 pieces of lemon zest in each chamber. Fill the chambers with water and freeze for at least 4 hours and up to 2 weeks. To serve, pop the cubes out of the tray, place them in glasses, and use to chill iced tea.

Minted Iced Tea Cubes

MAKES 12 CUBES

24 fresh mint leaves   3 cups brewed tea, at room temperature or chilled

Using a 12-cube ice cube tray, place 2 mint leaves in each chamber. Fill each chamber with the brewed tea and freeze for at least 4 hours and up to 2 weeks. To serve, pop the cubes out of the tray, place them in glasses, and use to chill iced tea.

Apricot Lime Sparkler

SERVES 4

When I'm hosting a lunch gathering, I love offering a light signature cocktail rather than presenting my guests with a ream of beverage options. (That demands way too much thinking on their parts!) This is one of my favorites: fruity, a little exotic, easy to make, and refreshing. It can be transformed into a nonalcoholic drink if you replace the sparkling wine with lemon-lime soda and a splash of seltzer (so you still have bubbles, because bubbles make any occasion more fun, don't they?).

½ cup sugar

1 lime

1 cup apricot juice

2 cups sparkling wine (Cava, Prosecco, sparkling Pinot Grigio, or another sparkling wine)

Place the sugar in a shallow bowl. Cut 5 lime wedges. Use 1 lime wedge to wet the rim of each of 4 glasses. Dip the wet rims into the sugar to coat them. Turn the glasses right side up. Add a lime wedge to each glass. Pour ¼ cup of the apricot juice into each glass, then top it off with ½ cup of the sparkling wine, and serve.

Prosecco with Mango & Strawberries

SERVES 4

I love combining fruit and fruit juice with bubbly—here's another way to do just that!

8 strawberries, green part removed,
    chopped into ¼-inch pieces

1 cup mango juice

2 cups chilled Prosecco

Place the strawberries in a medium bowl, pour the mango juice over them, and let sit for 15 minutes in the refrigerator to macerate. Divide the mixture among 4 Champagne flutes, then top each glass with ½ cup of the Prosecco and serve immediately.

Lunchtime Wine

I don't have a glass of wine with lunch every day, though I have European friends who do! Every now and then, though, I love a leisurely lunch paired with wine. For me, lunch isn't the time for big, bold reds or heavy, oaky whites (but if that's what you love, go for it—I think the most important rule of choosing wines is that you should like what you drink!). Here are a few wines to think about next time you consider opening a bottle at lunchtime.

CAVA: If you don't want to pay for French Champagne at lunchtime, try the much less expensive Spanish cava. The method by which it's made is the same, and it's dry and crisp. You could also try a California sparkling wine.

PROSECCO: This is an Italian sparkling wine that's bubbly and fun and pairs well with just about everything.

SPARKLING ROSÉ: This sparkling wine is fuller-bodied and fuller-flavored than cava or prosecco. I love it with stronger dishes like roasted meats and acidic dishes that have tomato in them.

PINOT GRIGIO: This light-bodied Italian wine tastes great with fish, chicken, and pasta dishes.

CHABLIS: Fans of the Chardonnay grape who don't want a heavy Chardonnay with lunch could sample some French Chablis. It's made with Chardonnay grapes, but typically lighter and much less oaky than California Chardonnay.

SAUVIGNON BLANC: No matter what country it's from, this refreshing white wine is lovely with seafood, since it has notes of citrus, especially grapefruit.

ROSÉ: Pink wine is very chic right now, and for good reason. A crisp, dry rosé is light and refreshing, and yet it has some wonderful complexity too. It also pairs really well with most foods.

PINOT NOIR: There's a huge variety of Pinot Noir to be found, but it's generally a lighter-bodied red, which I think is lovely for lunch.

CHIANTI: This light and fruity red wine pairs well with almost any Italian-inspired dish.

BEAUJOLAIS: Generally made from Gamay grapes, this French wine is meant for drinking while it's young and fresh, so it never has time to develop a big red profile. Beaujolais Nouveau is usually consumed two months after it is released, when it's not more than a year or two old in the bottle.

GRENACHE: These red wines are friendly and fruity. They're great with sandwiches and hearty soups, and can handle strong-flavored foods like blue cheese and beef.

Index

Note: Page references in *italics* indicate photographs.